GW01374736

A History of the Church
and Parish of St. Martin's Dorking

St. Martin's Church, the town and surrounding countryside, seen from South Street, a photograph taken c1900.

A History of the Church and Parish of St. Martin's Dorking

edited by
Alexandra Wedgwood

Published by the Friends of St. Martin's
1990

Copyright©
The Trustees of the Friends of St. Martin's
1990

Cover: stained glass of 1867 by William Wailes with scenes from the life of St. Martin, a detail from the south-east window of the chancel.

ISBN 0 9516097 0 X

Printed by Tappenden Print, Billingshurst, West Sussex RH14 9EZ

Contents

	List of Illustrations	ii
	Acknowledgements	iv
	Preface by the Vicar and the Methodist Minister	v
1.	*The Church in Dorking and District* (A. Wedgwood)	1
2.	The History of the Church and Parish to the Nineteenth Century (V. Ettlinger)	3
3.	The Intermediate and Present Churches (A. Wedgwood); Furnishings (A. Wedgwood); Vestments, frontals and kneelers (J. Edwards); The Organ (M. Ellis); The Bells (E. Clear).	21
4.	Some Priests and People: The Revds. James and William Henry Joyce (J. M. Foster); William Henry Forman and Elizabeth Forman (P. Bennett); Canon Chichester (E. Clear); Lily, Duchess of Marlborough (E. D. Mercer).	55
5.	Music at St. Martin's (M. Ellis)	69
6.	Kenneth Evans and Jack Roundhill (C. B. Carr)	81
7.	Methodism in Dorking (M. G. Brigham)	96
	Appendix A — Places of Worship in Dorking	110
	Appendix B — Methodist Ministers stationed in Dorking	112
8.	St. Barnabas Church, Ranmore (S. Pratt)	114
	Appendix C — Rectors of St. Barnabas, Ranmore	125
9.	Pixham Church (L. Parnell)	126
10.	The Shared Church from 1976 (M. J. Farrant)	140

Appendices
    I Vicars 149
   II Assistant Clergy 150
  III Churchwardens 153
  IV Organists 156

Sources and Bibliography 159

Index 161

i

List of Illustrations

Frontis		Dorking: church and town c1900 *(David Knight)*.
Page	vi	The cover of the parish magazine of Christ Church, Epsom Common, February 1923, with photograph of Neville Stiff *(Revd. Mark Wilson)*.
Page	5	Map of the ancient parish of Dorking *(Beryl Higgins)*.
Page	6	The architectural development of St. Martin's Church *(Beryl Higgins)*.
Page	7	The exterior of the medieval church c1830 *(Dorking Museum)*.
Page	7	Model of the medieval church *(Dorking Museum)*.
Page	8	Lych-gate to the medieval church, 1829 *(St. Martin's Church records deposited at Surrey Record Office, Guildford)*.
Page	8	View of the interior of the medieval church, 1829 *(St. Martin's Church records deposited at Surrey Record Office, Guildford)*.
Page	23	Competition drawing for the Intermediate Church, 1835 *(Dorking Museum)*.
Page	23	View of the exterior of the Intermediate Church, c1855 *(Dorking Museum)*.
Page	24	View of the interior of the medieval chancel, 1839 *(St. Martin's Church records deposited at Surrey Record Office, Guildford)*.
Page	24	View of the interior of the Intermediate Church, 1839 *(St. Martin's Church records deposited at Surrey Record Office, Guildford)*.
Page	25	Designs for the Forman chancel by H. Woodyer, 1866 *(Surrey Record Office, Guildford)*.
Page	25	Exterior of the Forman chancel, c1870 *(N. E. C. Molyneux)*.
Page	26	The stained glass of 1867 in the east window of the chancel.
Page	29	Plan of St. Martin's church, surveyed 1990 *(Hugh Pite)*.
Page	30	View of the exterior of the church, 1978 *(RCHM England)*.
Page	33	View of the interior of the church, c1910 *(St. Martin's Church records deposited at Surrey Record Office, Guildford)*.
Page	34	Stained glass of 1888 in the south aisle.
Page	34	Stained glass of 1894 in the north aisle.
Page	37	Wall panel of 1898 in the south aisle.
Page	37	Memorial to Henry Harman Young in the north aisle.
Page	38	Reredos of 1905 in the Lady Chapel.
Page	41	Central panel of white altar frontal of 1868.
Page	41	Detail from the gold and white festival frontal of 1969.
Page	42	Bells nos. 2, 3, 4 and 5 ready to ring, 1990.
Page	42	Mr. Dodd with lady bellringers, c1915 *(Dorking Museum)*.
Page	59	The Right Revd. Samuel Wilberforce, c1864 *(National Portrait Gallery)*.
Page	60	The clergy at St. Martin's in the early 1880's *(St. Martin's Church records deposited at Surrey Record Office, Guildford)*.
Page	65	Canon Chichester, c1915 *(St. Martin's Church records deposited at Surrey Record Office, Guildford)*.
Page	66	Memorial to Lily, Duchess of Marlborough, 1910.
Page	75	View of the interior of the church looking north-east, showing the organ case of 1868 and that of 1932/3 *(Norman Gibbs)*.
Page	75	St. Martin's clergy, choir, organists and servers, 1951 *(William Cole)*.
Page	76	Memorial to Dr. Ralph Vaughan Williams, 1961.

Page 76	Dr. William Cole *(Norman Gibbs)*.
Page 79	S.P.G. Pageant in the Vicarage garden, 1938 *(Dulcie Pickford)*.
Page 79	The Revd. George Adams *(Dorking Museum)*.
Page 79	The Revd. A. E. Robins *(Dulcie Pickford)*.
Page 80	St. Martin's Youth Fellowship c1939 *(Evelyn Gibbs)*.
Page 80	Canon E. J. Newill *(Dorking Museum)*.
Page 80	The Revd. Anthony Weigall *(Dulcie Pickford)*.
Page 89	View from the chancel looking west during alterations, 1965 *(Dorking Advertiser)*.
Page 90	The Parish Conference at Netley House, Gomshall, 1971 *(Pam Hunter)*.
Page 99	The first Methodist Meeting Place, Back Lane, c1800 *(Dorking Methodist Church archives)*.
Page 100	Edith Corderoy *('The Dorking British School')*.
Page 100	Charles Degenhardt *(Helen Rivers)*.
Page 105	The Methodist Church, South Street, 1959 *(Dorking Methodist Church archives)*.
Page 106	The Revd. Ronald Rawlings with the Revd. Jack Roundhill, 1973 *(Dorking Advertiser)*.
Page 117	Exterior view of St. Barnabas Church, Ranmore *(M. Jewkes)*.
Page 117	Interior view of St. Barnabas Church, Ranmore *(Dorking Museum)*.
Page 118	Memorial plaque to George, first Baron Ashcombe.
Page 118	Portrait of Henry Archibald Cubitt *(Lord Ashcombe)*.
Page 118	Portrait of Henry, second Baron Ashcombe *(Lord Ashcombe)*.
Page 119	The altarpiece in the Cubitt chapel, St. Barnabas Church, Ranmore.
Page 120	Holy Communion at St. Barnabas Church, Ranmore, on 21 January, 1990.
Page 129	Old Iron Room, Pixham *('Pixham 1862-1912')*.
Page 129	St. Martin's Church Room, Pixham *('Pixham 1862-1912')*.
Page 130	Interior of Pixham Church *('Pixham 1862-1912')*.
Page 131	Designs by E. Lutyens for Pixham Church *(British Architectural Library)*.
Page 131	Pixham Church choir, 1951 *(Pixham Church archives)*.
Page 132	"Godspell" in Pixham Church, 1987 *(Lynn Parnell)*.
Page 132	Holy Communion at Pixham Church on 4 February 1990.
Page 141	Harvest Festival in St. Martin's, 1978 *(Margaret Pantrey)*.
Page 142	Induction of the Revd. Martyn Farrant on 7 May, 1983 *(Dorking Advertiser)*.
Page 143	View of the Christian Centre, 1990.
Page 144	The 9.30 am Anglican Service at St. Martin's on 28 January 1990.
Page 147	The 11.00 am Methodist Service at St. Martin's on 28 January 1990.
Page 148	The Shared Service at St. Martin's on 25 March 1990.
Page 157	Samuel Dendy, churchwarden 1733, and Samuel Dendy, churchwarden 1778.
Page 157	Arthur Powell, churchwarden 1871.
Page 157	George Smith Brown, churchwarden 1918-39 *(Mrs. Tyler)*.
Page 157	Churchwardens Norman Gibbs and Ben Trim, 1986. *(E. Clear)*
Page 158	The present organist, Martin Ellis, 1990.

Acknowledgements

I am glad to acknowledge the role of the Vicar, the Revd. Martyn Farrant, for the initial impetus behind this book, and I am grateful for the encouragement and support that he, the Methodist Minister, John Hope, and the other Trustees of the Friends of St. Martin's Church, Michael Brigham, Edgar Christian, Michael Light, Iain Macleod and, most particularly, the chairman, Brian Carr, have given to this project.

I wish to thank the contributors, who have all been a pleasure to work with. Two of them, however, must be singled out for their outstanding help over and above their own sections. I have consistently been able to rely on the invaluable experience and knowledge of Vivien Ettlinger, who has also produced the index, and Ethel Clear has always been willing to make the resources of the Dorking Museum and Library available to all the contributors. The research work accumulated during this project will all be placed in the Museum.

Patricia Bennett has kindly provided the bibliography. The primary research for this book has mostly been done at Surrey Record Office, and we have all greatly appreciated the help of Dr. David Robinson and his staff at County Hall, Kingston and Sheila Himsworth and her staff at Guildford Muniment Room. Many special photographs have been taken for this book and I wish to thank Barry Edwards for his details of the buildings, Dennis Hooker for his pictures of the churches at worship, James Berry-Clarke for the items in the Dorking Museum, and Keith Harding for copying many old photographs; also Beryl Higgins and Hugh Pite who have drawn new maps and plans.

Many people have helped and we are very grateful to them. Particular thanks are due to Lord Ashcombe, the Revd. John Bird, Mrs. P. G. Buckingham, Peter Bunn, Leslie Castle, Marguerite Chalcraft, John Coombes, Doncaster Borough Council Archivist, Robert Edmondson, Carel Elias, Anne Elphick, Mr. and Mrs. Michael Elphick, Peter Essex, Bishop Kenneth Evans, Wendy Evans, Mr. and Mrs Norman Gibbs, Pat Hill, Pam Hunter, Sister Isobel Joy, David Knight, Charles Macrorie, Doris Mercer, N. E. C. Molyneux, Margaret Pantry, Dulcie Pickford, Fay Prickett, Nigel Proctor, Alan Pullinger, Jim Ralph, Helen Rivers, Canon Jack Roundhill, Shropshire County Record Office, Rosemary Spiers, Joan and Audrey Stampe, Philip Storr-Venter, Brian Tucker and the Revd. Mark Wilson.

I undertook this project almost light-heartedly, and I have been astonished at the amount of work involved. My admiration for the author of the forerunner of this book, Neville Stiff, is very great, as are my thanks to my long-suffering husband.

Alexandra Wedgwood
June 1990

Preface

We are proud of the fact that St. Martin's Church has a long history and that the four churches (maybe more) to have been on this site span many hundreds of years. Our Christian faith has a long ancestry; and we are greatly blessed not only because the present St. Martin's is such a fine building but also, and chiefly, because we have such a rich heritage.

This heritage includes the Holy Scriptures, loved, acted upon, preserved and delivered safely to our day. Also we rejoice in the heritage of the Ministry of Word and Sacrament — a long and devoted line of clergy who have brought the Things of God into the lives of the folk of this town. Specially we affirm the heritage of the tradition of faith and holiness of life entered into joyfully by God's people throughout the history of this place.

In the Letter to the Ephesians we read that we are "built upon the foundation laid by the apostles and prophets, and Christ Jesus himself is the foundation-stone." (2.20). When school children have a conducted tour of St. Martin's they are always fascinated to see the early foundations in the crypt. But we are always at pains to point out that the real foundation of the Church is Jesus Christ himself. The faith may be historical (and indeed it is based firmly upon historical events) but it is also a faith for living today.

So we commend this book to you, and hope that it will both help your understanding of the Church in this place throughout the ages, and also that the Faith may give you a firm footing for your life and that the Love of Jesus may enrich all your days.

Martyn Farrant and John Hope

Christ Church, Epsom Common,
(with S. MICHAEL'S)
PARISH MAGAZINE.

To be issued for the present every other month.

FEB. & MAR., 1923.   No. 11. (N.G.J.S.)   Price 2d.

In Affectionate Memory of

Neville George Joseph Stiff,

Fourth Vicar of Christ Church, Epsom Common,
who entered into a fuller life on Sunday, 28th January, 1923.
Interred Epsom Cemetery.

Churchwardens.
Mr. H. W. ABSALOM,
Breamore,
Station Road.

Mr. T. E. WARE,
The Hatchgate,
Ashtead.

Organist
Mr. G. E. GOOD,
High Street.

By courtesy of the "Epsom Herald."

Neville Stiff, author of The Church in Dorking and District *(1912), a photograph of c1922 shown on the cover of his parish magazine following his death.*

Chapter 1

The Church in Dorking and District

The July issue of the Parish magazine of 1912 announced the imminent publication of the book, *The Church in Dorking and District*. Its author, one of the curates, Neville G. J. Stiff, had only arrived in Dorking the previous year, and so he had got to work very quickly on what has become a classic work of reference, in constant use by local historians. 'What does Stiff say?' is a common cry. He is the inspiration for the present book.

He had been educated at King's College, London and was ordained deacon in the diocese of London in 1904 and priest in 1905. His first curacy was at All Saints, Clapton Park, and here in 1907 he published his first and only other book, *Our Neighbourhood, Our Parish and Our Church*. This was a record of the formation of the parish, its life and the history of the area in one of the leafier parts of Hackney, and it was clearly a success. He said: 'The very kind reception that this effort received from Clapton folk and others made me undertake a similar little book about Dorking Parish Church.'

He left Clapton in 1909 but, before coming to Dorking, he crossed London to Hanwell, an area north of Osterley Park, where he was priest in charge of St. Mark's church. He remarked himself that it was unusual for London clergy to come to Dorking. In view of his subsequent history it seems probable that Neville Stiff was already suffering from ill-health and was looking for a less polluted place in which to work.

When he arrived at St. Martin's in 1911 he joined a staff of two other curates under the vicar, Canon Chichester, and this perhaps enabled him to have the time to write this thorough, accurate and extremely interesting history. For the medieval period Stiff mostly relied on the recently published *Victoria County History of Surrey*, and the major nineteenth century histories, such as those by Brayley, and Manning and Bray. Much of this material has of course now been proved inadequate by subsequent primary research and, for instance, the early part of Stiff's list of vicars has been substantially altered. From the eighteenth century onwards, however, he used many original sources, including the Rural Deanery book, the parish registers, rate books and vestry minutes. For more recent periods he must have talked to many local people, and used the Surrey newspapers and parish magazines. It is amusing to note that in his book on Clapton he laments how difficult it is to find old parish magazines, a cry that must be repeated in 1990! Although it is odd to discover that he made mistakes about the Formans of Pippbrook, he is generally to be trusted. Stiff was most resourceful in finding illustrations for his book, particularly the excellent portraits. The result was impressive and the July 1912 Parish Magazine stated: 'It is urgent that we should obtain more subscribers before it is in circulation. The book will be a little larger than originally intended and the expenses will be very heavy. We shall be very grateful if all friends of the Parish Church will order one copy now, price 2/6.'

Stiff did not remain in Dorking long to enjoy the success of his book. From here he spent a year with the registry staff of the diocese of Winchester and then in 1914 he went to Southampton, a change that again may have been due to reasons of health. Until 1921 he was the incumbent of St. Agnes, Hampton Park, in which year he became vicar of Christ Church, Epsom Common, and within two years he was dead. A most affectionate memoir of him written by his verger appeared in the centenary booklet of 1976 for Christ Church:

Neville Stiff 'was a tall man with a crew cut — a most unusual thing in those days. We knew him for his gaiety, humour and godliness — qualities that always seem to go together — and yet I have never known a man suffer from asthma as much as he did. He would ask me to go over to the Vicarage and lend him my arm so that he could walk to the Church. And after the service he would ask me to close the Vestry door so that no-one saw him as he struggled for breath. His Sunday evening services were such that his reputation quickly spread throughout Epsom and it was difficult to get a seat unless you were there early. His sermons were not emotional but they moved us deeply . . . Neville Stiff would have been a great man in whatever age he had lived and he would have been able to adjust to the many changes coming about in the Church today . . . Despite his great handicap, he was always about on his bicycle, visiting his people, exhorting and teaching them. They were wonderful days at Christ Church — but oh, so short a period!'

In his book about Dorking Stiff appears as a delightful man, with a strong faith and clear opinions, convinced of the rightness of the High Church position within the Church of England. In view of the subsequent history of St. Martin's it is particularly encouraging to read his final prophetic words: 'We wish all work done in Christ's name to prosper; we recognise the good done by our fellow-Christians who worship apart from us; we admire their energy, and we believe in a future and lasting reunion.'

Chapter 2

History of the Church and Parish to the Nineteenth Century

Parish and Diocese

The parish of Dorking was probably once part of a much larger ecclesiastical division owned by the Saxon kings and served by a community of priests from a mother church or minster at Leatherhead. By the time of the Norman conquest this large area had been sub-divided and the estate or manor of Dorking had become a separate parish, with its own church, embracing an area bounded by Betchworth on the east and Wotton and Ockley on the west, and stretching from Bookham and Mickleham southward to the Sussex border.

Under the Normans the population of south-east England expanded rapidly, and by the mid-12th century a chapel-of-ease, the Capella de Ewekene, had been built to serve the tenants in the southern part of the manor. By the 14th century the independent parish of Capel was established, leaving the major part of the manor and township of Dorking in the original parish, and so it remained until the 19th century. Then economic prosperity and the spread of population to the home counties led to massive residential development of the neighbourhood and again made it necessary to build more churches, each serving a newly created parish.

The ancient common of Holmwood was the first to be affected and in 1838 the large parish of St. Mary Magdalene was created out of parts of Dorking and Capel parishes, only to lose its western sector in 1848 to be united with small areas of Ockley and Wotton and become the parish for the newly built church of Christ Church, Coldharbour. This was followed in 1852 by Holy Trinity, Westcott, for the inhabitants of the expanding village lying to the west of the town. By 1857 the needs of new house-owners in the south of the town and the desire of some parishioners of St. Martin's for a more Evangelical form of worship, led to the foundation of the new parish of St. Paul. Then, in 1860, by combining parts of Dorking, Mickleham, Great and Little Bookham and Effingham, the parish of Ranmore was established around the church of St. Barnabas, built by George Cubitt, later Lord Ashcombe, to serve the small community surrounding his Denbies estate. Still the population grew, and finally in 1874 the northern half of Holmwood was detached to form the parish of St. John the Evangelist, North Holmwood, for the convenience of the residents on the outskirts of the town.

The diocese in which Dorking lay for the greater part of its history was established by Bishop Birinus after converting the West Saxons in about A.D. 634. Winchester cathedral was founded about fourteen years later as the ecclesiastical centre for the kingdom of Wessex, and numbered amongst its bishops have been many distinguished men, prominent in church and state. The name best remembered locally is that of Samuel Wilberforce, bishop from 1869-1873, who laid the foundation stone of the tower of the present church, and whose untimely death a few weeks later in a riding accident at Evershed's Rough, Abinger, led to its completion as the Bishop Wilberforce Memorial Tower.

The Bishops of Winchester probably visited their flocks occasionally for confirmations and ordinations, but they were busy men with a vast diocese to oversee. Direct responsibility for Dorking and the other Surrey churches in the diocese had been delegated since Norman times to the Archdeacons of Surrey, and from the 14th century the parish was administered as part of a sub-division, the deanery of Stoke-by-Guildford. This was further divided in 1858 and St. Martin's became a parish in the deanery of South East Stoke, re-entitled Dorking in 1878. Both Archdeacons and Rural Deans made periodic visitations to report on the condition of the church and the conduct of its clergy.

By the end of the 19th century the enormous diocese of Winchester was no longer administratively viable, and in 1927 Dorking, with the other churches of West Surrey, passed into the newly created diocese of Guildford.

The Building

As with so many churches in the Middle Ages, Dorking's was usually referred to simply as "the parish church", though a 12th century deed suggests that it was dedicated at that time to St. Mary. In fact John Aubrey recorded that it was so known in 1673, but he was probably confusing it with Reigate. Certainly it was St. Martin according to a will made in 1486, and the name begins to come into common use from that date.

A church at Dorking is first mentioned in the Domesday Book compiled in 1086, and it is reasonable to assume that it stood on approximately the same site as the present one. Excavations in the crypt under the nave in 1974 disclosed no remains of such a building, which may imply that this Saxo-Norman church was smaller and farther to the east, perhaps beneath the modern chancel.

Fortunately, the building which was totally demolished in the 19th century and is generally referred to as the medieval church, was recorded by a number of artists and writers during its last days, so making it possible to attempt a reconstruction of the various stages of its development. The building appears to have originated in the mid-12th century, a time when many wealthy land-owners were founding or refurbishing churches on their estates, primarily as a pious act for the benefit of their immortal souls, but also of course contributing to the welfare of their tenants. Constructed of flint and chalk with a Horsham stone roof, it was cruciform with a central tower, and had a distinctive north transept with pilaster buttresses, and lancet windows, one of which pierced the central buttress. It was entered through a west porch.

Improvements to the nave were made in the early 13th century, and then, in the 14th century, the church underwent major alterations. Low, narrow side aisles were added to the nave, a clerestory constructed and many new windows were inserted, including a five-light one at the east end, leaving the exterior of the building much as it appears in later drawings. The south porch, which by the 19th century as a result of the build-up of graves, was on a level halfway between the church and the churchyard, was probably added in the 15th century, by which time there were altars in both side aisles, that on the north dedicated to St. Mary and containing a painting of her, and that on the south to St. John.

Minor modifications were made over the years as fashion or necessity dictated: more

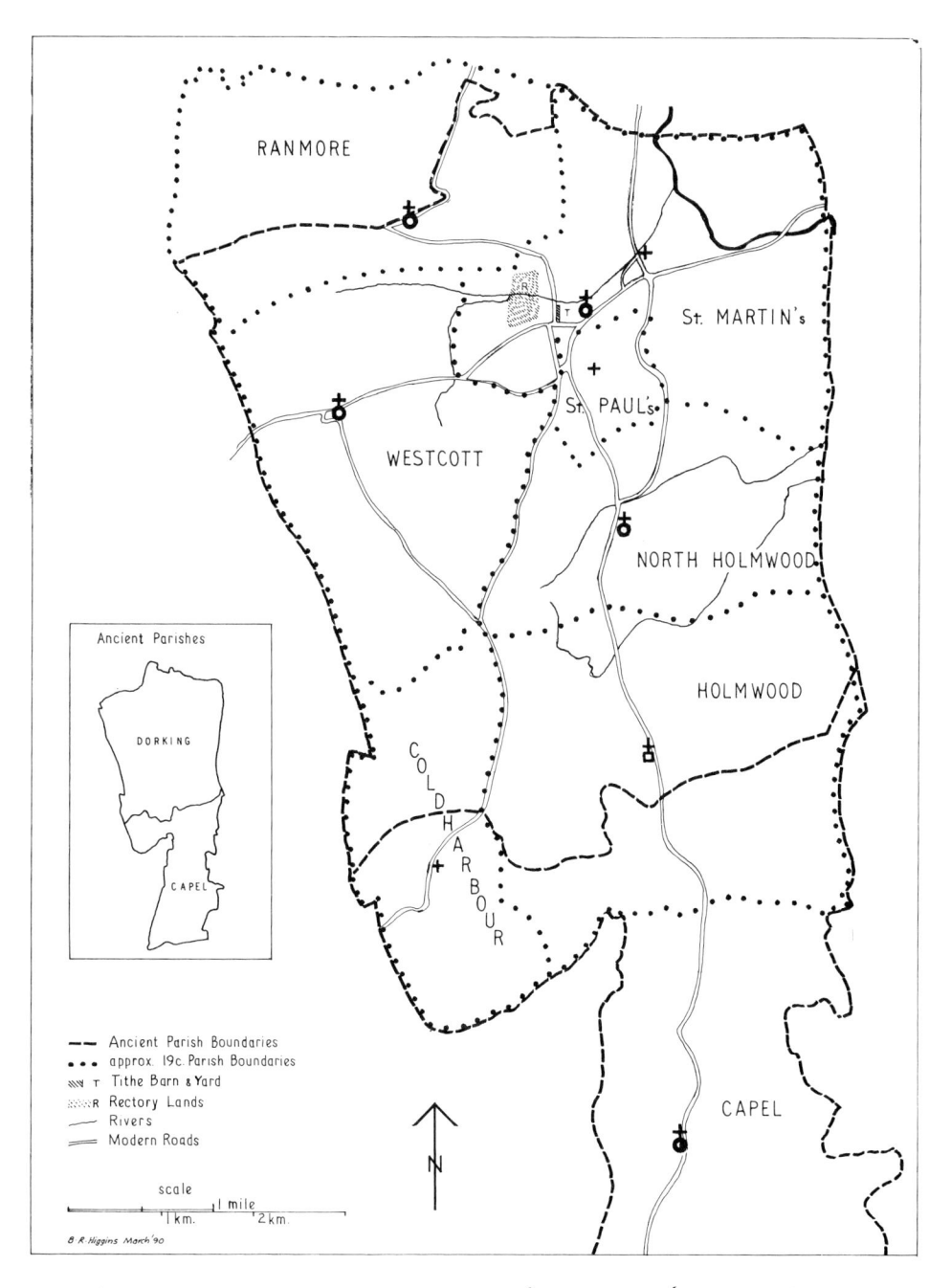

Approximate areas of Ecclesiastical Districts

Conjectural Saxon Church

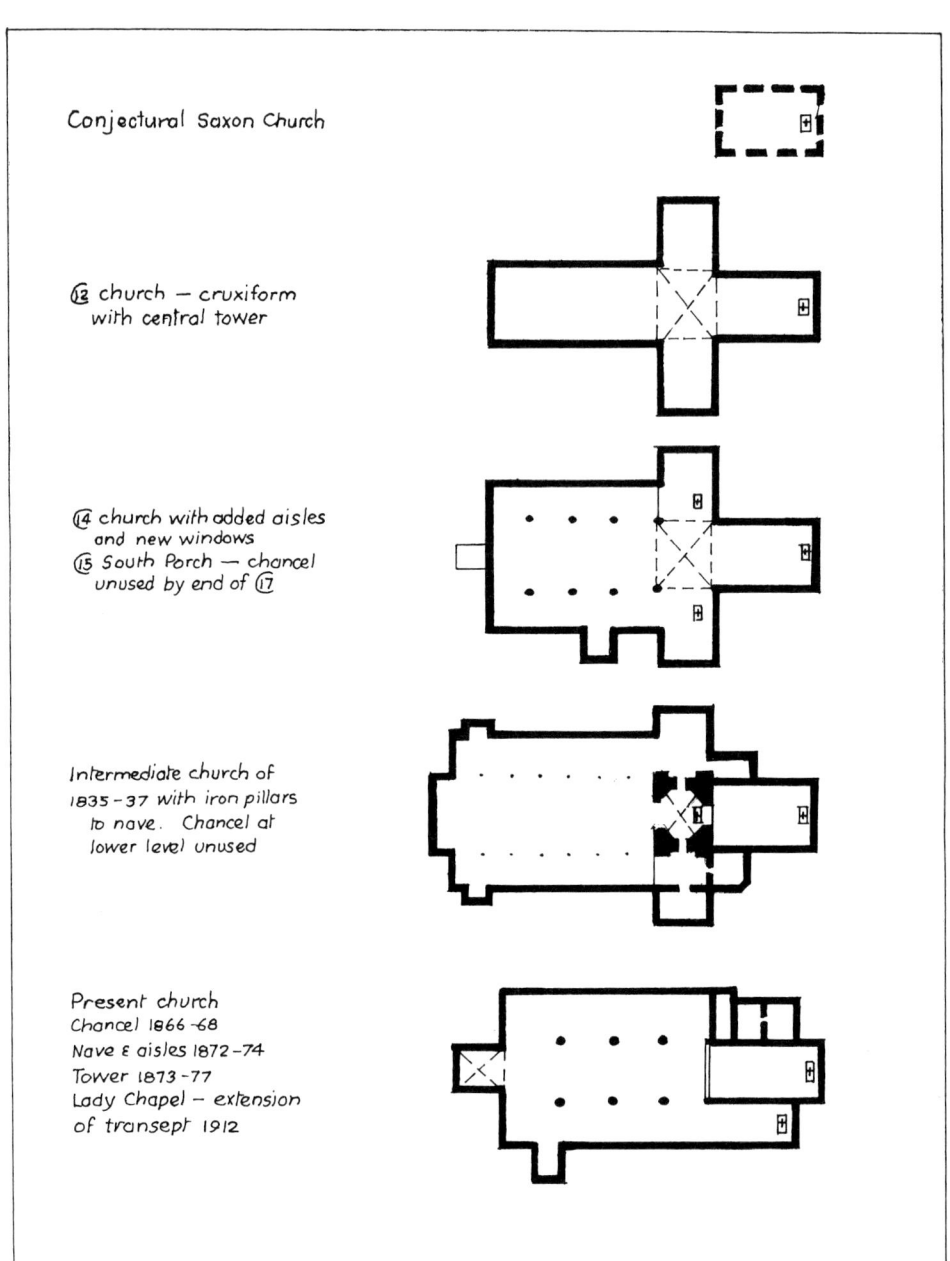

13 church — cruxiform with central tower

14 church with added aisles and new windows
15 South Porch — chancel unused by end of 17

Intermediate church of 1835-37 with iron pillars to nave. Chancel at lower level unused

Present church
Chancel 1866-68
Nave & aisles 1872-74
Tower 1873-77
Lady Chapel — extension of transept 1912

THE ARCHITECTURAL DEVELOPMENT of St. MARTIN's CHURCH

BRH 3/90

South-west view of the medieval church, an oil painting by John Beckett of c1830.

Model of the medieval church made by Bert Hall of Bovis Construction Ltd. in 1977, showing the north-west view.

The lych-gate to the medieval church, showing the view into the High Street, a watercolour by Edward Hassell, 1829.

View of the interior of the medieval church looking east, showing the solid screen in front of the central tower with the paintings of Moses and Aaron above and the monuments to Catherine Talbot and the Earl of Rothes below, a watercolour by Edward Hassell, 1829.

windows were added to the south aspect, parts of the stone roof were replaced with tiles, the tower needed attention on more than one occasion and in 1762 had to be strengthened with a buttress in its SE angle. Subsequent repairs to the fabric were made in more modern building materials like brick and cement.

The appearance of the medieval interior can only be conjectured but it is likely that a stone-flagged floor, unfurnished except for a font, would have stretched between whitewashed walls painted with biblical scenes. Further clues may be deduced from an inventory of church goods made in 1552. Attention would have been focussed on the copper gilt cross on the high altar, illuminated by a hanging lamp and candles in brass candlesticks. More candles would have shone before the effigies of the saints above the side altars, and the priest would have performed the offices wearing vestments of richly coloured velvet and satin. The altars would have been covered with painted cloths, chalices and other vessels of silver and brass would have gleamed in the candle light, and somewhere there was a clock.

It was to the interior that the post-medieval parishioners devoted their money and energies. The altars and anything else connected with Popish practices would almost certainly have been removed by the end of the 16th century and anything overlooked then would have gone in the Puritan reforms of the middle 1600s. It was probably not long before some pews were provided for the convenience of a congregation now committed to listening to lengthy sermons, and in 1637 a hexagonal wooden pulpit was installed in a central position on the north side of the nave. The blue and gilt panelled ceiling of the east end of the nave was probably part of the "beautification" recorded in 1674, but the solid partition between the nave and chancel described as having been covered in the early 19th century with sacred writings and "some strange painting, among which Moses and Aaron shone with peculiar uncouthness" seems more likely to have been constructed a little later. Certainly the royal coat of arms which can be seen in a contemporary painting over the entrance to the chancel is said to have been that of George II. In the 18th century a gallery was inserted over the west end of the nave to accommodate the band, and in time an irregular assortment of similar structures appeared over both side aisles, erected individually by wealthy parishioners for use as family pews. In 1756, for example, Henry Talbot of Chart Park obtained a vestry order permitting him not only to build a gallery in the north east corner, but also to divide the vestry room to provide him with a private passage and staircase to it.

It is not known when, or for that matter why, the chancel with its beautiful east window was virtually isolated. The emphasis on the pulpit rather than the altar may have been a contributory factor, and it is of note that St. Martin's apparently continued to use a plain communion table until the present chancel was built. In 1829, the Rural Dean reported that this table was inlaid with oilcloth, the cloth having been stolen some years before. Presumably the chancel was still used for celebrations of Holy Communion, and its walls were favoured for memorial tablets during the 17th, 18th and early 19th centuries.

It was clearly an interesting building but it did not survive the changing opinions of the 19th century. What happened at Dorking was, however, most unusual. In 1835 the nave, aisles and porches were demolished and replaced and the central tower and transepts altered. (*See* the Intermediate Church). In 1866 the medieval chancel was replaced by the present one and then, between 1872 and 1874, the Intermediate Church was demolished to make way for the one there today. *(See* the Present Church).

Patronage

Before the Conquest, the Manor of Dorking belonged to the Saxon royal family and it is probable that the church standing at Domesday was founded by one of them for the use of their tenants. After the death in 1075 of Edith, widow of Edward the Confessor, the whole estate passed to the Norman king, William, who owned it at Domesday, and it was granted by William Rufus in about 1088 to one of his barons, William de Warenne, Lord of Lewes and Earl of Surrey. Sometime between 1138 and 1147 Warenne's daughter-in-law, the Dowager Countess Isabel, granted the church of Dorking with its lands and tithes to the Cluniac Priory of St. Pancras, Lewes, and it seems likely that the lady was responsible for the 12th century reconstruction before so doing. In 1334 ownership of the church passed from Lewes to the Augustinian Prior and Convent of the Holy Cross, Reigate, who remained its patrons until the Reformation, when the religious houses were dissolved and their property and rights disposed of to lay proprietors as valuable marketable commodities.

The advowson and lands of the church of Dorking were granted in 1541 to Lord William Howard, later Lord Howard of Effingham, and they descended through his family to the Mordaunts who sold in 1677 to Sir John Parsons. They were subsequently conveyed to Sir John Hynde Cotton who sold in 1789 to the Lord of the Manor, Charles Howard, 11th Duke of Norfolk, owner at that time of the Deepdene. Unlike most of his family he had renounced the Roman Catholic faith and when he died in 1815 he was interred with great pomp in St. Martin's. His successors, who lived at Arundel, were of the old faith and gradually disposed of the rectorial tithes and land, finally selling the patronage of the church to George Cubitt in 1865.

Originally, churches were the personal property of their founders who appointed the priests to serve them, and this right of patronage or advowson was included in the grant to Lewes Priory. This allowed the Priory either to appoint a priest directly, or, as in Dorking, to nominate a rector, known sometimes as the parson. The rector was not obliged to be resident, or even to be in holy orders, in which case he could retain part of the income for himself but was expected to employ a concurrent vicar, an ordained minister, to carry out the pastoral duties in the parish.

The rector of Dorking had two main sources of income. He received the proceeds of cultivating or, more probably, leasing out the rectory or parsonage lands, most of which lay in a large block on either side of the Pippbrook to the north of the Westcott Road. He also received the Great Tithes which were levied on all the grain, hay and timber produced in the parish. These were collected in the tithe barn which stood in the parsonage yard at the corner of Church Street and Station Road, formerly Parsonage Lane. *(See* map).

Only three rectors of Dorking presented by Lewes Priory are known by name. The earliest was John de Warenne, probably an illegitimate son of the then Earl, whose institution in about 1294 is a blatant case of nepotism and corruption. Although at the same time he was a canon and prebendary of York and rector of the parishes of Dewsbury and Fishlake, he was never ordained priest and it was simply a means, inadequate it would seem, of providing him with an income. On several occasions the goods and tithes of the church of Dorking, said to be worth 100 marks a year, were ordered to be confiscated to pay his debts, and in 1310 he was actually excommunicated and the church placed under an interdict. This ecclesiastical punishment deprived the parishioners of all spiritual care, and it is quite likely that Dorking was without a vicar for a period.

John de Warenne had resigned by 1322 and was succeeded by John of Malmesbury, a worthier man who, though probably accepting the benefice to finance his career in church and government service, nevertheless installed a qualified vicar. After three years he exchanged the rectory of Dorking with Robert de Balne about whom little is known except that he died in 1341, by which time the advowson had passed from Lewes to Reigate Priory. Henceforth, the Priors themselves became the rectors by virtue of their office and they appointed the vicars, who had to be approved by the bishop. After the Reformation, the new lay proprietors assumed the role, and so Dorking remains a vicarage to this day.

The Clergy

The earliest recorded priest of Dorking was one William who witnessed two Lewes Priory charters in 1147, but with the possible exception of two clerks called Robert and William who appeared at the manor court in 1282, nothing is known of his successors until 1318. In that year, towards the end of the scandalous rectorship of John de Warenne, the induction of Henry de Habitone, on the personal presentation of the bishop, marked the beginning of a well documented succession of vicars (*see* list at Appendix I) and by this date the qualifications, duties and benefits attaching to the office had been regularised.

Late medieval vicars were required to be ordained priests so that they could administer the sacraments, they were expected to be resident and celibate and they had of course to be literate. In 1403 the living was actually held by a graduate, Robert Ketene, a highly regarded diocesan official who had been instrumental in founding Winchester College, to which he left his law library. The fact that he held several other livings simultaneously does unfortunately cast doubt on his single-minded attention to Dorking. The majority of vicars, however, though not all so well-educated, appear to have been resident, indeed active: in 1366 Walter Chapman was accused of poaching, though happily acquitted by public acclaim, while in 1395 Stephen Blancombe, who was perhaps less popular, was fined for assaulting two of his parishioners.

These vicars were entitled to a dwelling house with some land which they could work themselves or rent out, and to the Small Tithes which were levied on poultry, eggs, lambs, horticultural produce, craftsmen's profits etc. In addition, they received fees for burials and marriages, and on the death of a customary tenant of the manor they were entitled to his second-best beast, a perquisite known as a mortuary. (The best beast went to the lord, and there is an interesting case in the manor court in 1522 when the vicar was found to have taken the best one and had to return it.) This income was supposed to provide them with a living, with enough over to care for the poor and needy, and certainly there is no evidence to suggest that any Dorking vicars were impoverished. Several of them were apparently able to engage in property deals in the manor.

Rather more is known of the post-Reformation vicars, though the information is incomplete until relatively modern times. Celibacy was no longer insisted upon, and Stephen

Richman was already a married man with a family when he was instituted in 1572. They were well-educated men, mostly of the same social caste as the lesser gentry, and they appear to have taken the various changes in religious thinking in their stride, with the possible exception, in 1622, of Paul Clapham. He was an uncompromising cleric who later, as vicar of Farnham, was condemned by the Puritans as being "a man of very bad character who called the Parliament Rebels and Traitors and fled to the King's army". The next vicar, Samuel Cozens, who began his incumbency under James I, probably welcomed the Puritan innovations of the Commonwealth. The Trustees for Providing Maintenance for Preaching Ministers made him an allowance of £20 in 1656, and he had to be persuaded to use the re-introduced Book of Common Prayer in 1660. Perhaps fortunately, he died in 1661 and his curate Edward Nabbs, a man of similar views, left the parish. The succeeding vicar, Thomas Lea, reluctantly subscribed to the Act of Uniformity in 1662 and thus avoided ejection.

There are occasional references to curates in the 16th and 17th centuries, but the first evidence for their regular employment in the parish begins in 1725. (*See* Appendix II). It is possible that medieval vicars, particularly if they were non-resident, appointed assistant clergy and there are several early references to parish chaplains but some of these at least are likely to have been independent chantry priests. For a period after the Commonwealth outside ministers known as lecturers were invited by the parishioners to preach, and this practice may have been of particular benefit during the early 18th century when two vicars, Henry Lodge and Philip Walton, held Dorking in plurality with Mickleham.

It has not so far been possible to locate the original glebe house and land granted by the founder as part of the benefice, though there are indications that it may have stood on the north side of Church Street. Early vicars are recorded as living or owning property in various parts of the town, but by the 17th century they were permanently established in a vicarage at the south-western corner of North Street and Church Street which they occupied for two hundred years. By the early 19th century however this building was in an advanced state of dilapidation, and a house in South Street where Mays garage stands today, was taken over as a temporary vicarage. More suitable premises were found in 1839 when the fine house at the end of Vincent Lane was bought from Mr. W. J. Denison of Denbies. Money for the purchase of this property and a few adjoining acres belonging to the Duke of Norfolk came from the sale of the ancient vicarage, topped up by a large loan from Queen Anne's Bounty. The house served as St. Martin's Vicarage until 1986 when it was vacated in favour of its stable-block, now converted to suit the needs of a modern vicar and his family.

Schools

It was quite usual for parish priests to supplement their salaries by giving lessons to the children of parishioners, and in the days of cramped, ill-lit dwelling houses, a quiet corner of the church would sometimes be devoted to the purpose. How early this practice started in Dorking is not known, but by the late 17th century the north transept of the church was being used as a reading and writing school, and the south as a Latin school. By 1804 the latter was full of lumber and presumably pupils requiring higher education were receiving it at more suitable establishments. A school of some sort was still being conducted in the north transept, and perhaps continued until 1818 when a National School for boys and girls of the parish was built outside the north-west corner of the present churchyard. In 1862 this school was moved to West Street, and now as St Martin's First and Middle School it has found yet another home off Ranmore Road on the fringe of the town.

The original building served a number of purposes including that of a creche and was finally demolished in 1989 as part of the St Martin's Walk development scheme.

The Church's Place in the Community

For most people in the Middle Ages the church represented the supreme authority for conduct in this life, and the promise of hope for the next. Naturally, it was the centre of religious life where the parishioners would go to hear mass and the occasional homily, illustrated perhaps by reference to the wall paintings. They would take their children there to be baptised, and this need for water may partly explain the well which still exists in the crypt under the west end of St Martin's. Marriages and other contracts were solemnised, often in the porch. Burials took place, some, according to contemporary wills, inside the building. In 1464 a convicted thief took sanctuary there, before fleeing the realm.

But more than this, the church was the community centre for the parish. In bad weather public gatherings, possibly even the manor court, could take advantage of its shelter, and alms-raising festivities known as church ales may have enlivened it from time to time. Official notices were posted in the porch and proclamations of stray animals and other matters of local and national importance were made by the priest.

Although the rector was supposed to maintain the chancel, the upkeep of the nave fell upon the parishioners and the successive building developments prove that the people of Dorking honoured their obligations. Their contributions continued even after death, and many wills contained bequests to the church, some specifying the actual purpose to which the legacy should be put. In 1434 Henry Wolford left 10 marks to repair the belfry, and in 1490 Richard Wode allocated 6s 8d for repairing a glass window on the west side. Others left money to maintain the altar lights.

The effects of the Reformation were felt in Dorking no less than elsewhere. The rectory lands were confiscated and sold to lay proprietors who also acquired the right to appoint the vicar, although unlike some parishes, successive patrons appear to have behaved honourably and there is no record of an unfit or inadequately paid incumbent. English replaced Latin and services were conducted according to the new prayer book in a church now stripped bare of any idolatrous statues or paintings. But above all, the authority of the church had been challenged and with the spread of Protestant thinking, its influence in local affairs began to diminish.

Puritanism was apparently not in favour in the parish in 1620 when William Mullins, a West Street shoemaker, sailed with his family on the Mayflower, but by the Commonwealth period there does not seem to have been any local opposition to the new forms of worship. The vicar, who had been instituted in 1624, continued to conduct baptisms and burials but now preached every Sunday from the new pulpit which had become the focal point of the church. However, by Act of Parliament in 1653, marriages had become purely civil ceremonies and, after the publication of banns on three market days, were performed by Lawrence Marsh, a leading figure in the town, or one of his fellow J.P.s, probably in their private dwellings. The contracts were then recorded in the parish register by a parish clerk who was now answerable to Parliament. In the brief period from 1653 to 1661, Dorking had two such sworn Parish Registrars, John Hamon and Thomas Hill, but after the Restoration the responsibility for maintaining the registers returned once more to the vicar.

A small group of Roman Catholic gentry who had settled in the town, perhaps attracted by the presence of the Hon. Charles Howard, who lived at the Deepdene from 1652 until his death in 1713, kept a low and discreet profile. They attended the parish church when obliged to and some were even buried in the chancel.

There is also evidence that some noted dissenting clergy were active in the locality, and when, on the Restoration of Charles II, worship in the Church of England returned to a less austere form, a number of parishioners preferred to practise their religion in groups or conventicles meeting in their own homes. For a time such meetings were illegal and many local people were prosecuted at the Quarter Sessions for unlawful assembly, but in spite of this by 1669 there were four regular conventicles meeting in the neighbourhood.

According to estimates made for a religious census in 1676, the parish contained 200 nonconformists and 18 Roman Catholics out of a total of 1218 possible churchgoers, proportions well above the average for Surrey, and by 1725 the number of nonconformists had risen to 300 although the comparable figures were not recorded.

The Congregationalists were the first to take advantage of the 1689 Act of Toleration to set up an official meeting place in the town, and their example was soon followed by the Quakers. These buildings were noted by a contributor to the Gentleman's Magazine in 1763, who went on to say that "Dissenters are numerous but live in great harmony with members of the Established Church". By the end of the century the Methodists, too, had their own meeting house. *(See* Chapter 7).

In 1851 another religious census was conducted by Parliament although, unlike the civil census, it was not compulsory and encountered some opposition from the Church of England on the grounds that it intruded on privacy. Ministers from all the neighbouring churches and chapels duly made their returns, but unfortunately the vicar of St Martin's, the Revd. W.H. Joyce, declined to co-operate. However, it must have been obvious that by this date, although the total population was rising rapidly, the proportion of townspeople attending their parish church or looking to it for spiritual guidance was greatly reduced.

The Church's Role as a Secular Authority

During the Middle Ages local affairs were regulated through the Dorking manor court at the will of the lord or according to custom, while church business was managed by churchwardens who were elected by the parishioners. With the breakdown of the manorial system and the growth of central control under the Tudors, the government needed local authorities to implement their ordinances, and they turned to the parishes. The first parish clerk of Dorking to be mentioned by name was Robert Stapleton in 1496, and when in 1538 it became obligatory to keep registers of baptisms, marriages and burials, this office became essential. (Dorking is fortunate in having an almost complete series of registers from their inception.)

An Act of 1555 made parishes responsible for the highways and forced them to elect

Surveyors, and following the Elizabethan Poor Laws at the end of the century, churchwardens had also to take on the duties of Overseers of the Poor and deal with the vast masses of old, infirm and unemployed whose growing numbers had become a national problem. As the responsiblities of these parochial officers increased they had to meet regularly, generally in the vestry, by which name they became known. The earliest surviving minutes of Dorking Vestry date from the mid 18th century and contain instances of a variety of matters.

Naturally they were concerned with the maintenance of the church fabric and upkeep of the churchyard, and with employing the clerk, beadle and sexton and other officials and regulating the ringing of the bells, appointing visiting preachers, and granting planning permission for new monuments. As well as this, they were expected to set and collect the Poor Rate and apply it to the running of the Workhouse and any outside relief that was necessary, whilst ensuring that anyone who did not have a valid claim to residence in the parish was expelled. They had to fill vacancies in the almshouses and administer the various charities and allocate the proceeds appropriately, which could involve them in anything from distributing clothes and bread to setting up a poor boy as an apprentice, or even sending him to sea to cure him of a skin complaint.

Since the Middle Ages parish churches had been required to store fire-fighting equipment for public use, and it is satisfactory to note that in 1763 Dorking Vestry resolved to buy one and a half dozen buckets for this purpose, perhaps to be drawn at the well in the west end of the church which had been repaired the year before. Other duties were less traditional, as for instance a concern for public health and in 1788 dogs were ordered to be restrained because of an outbreak of what was described as madness. In 1767 inoculation against small-pox was regarded with suspicion and declared a public nuisance, and in 1833 it was again rejected, this time on the grounds that there were not enough cases, although rather surprisingly, the Vestry had ten years earlier authorised an experiment in "Acupuncturation" on a rheumatism sufferer.

The parish officers and other prominent townsmen who served on these Vestries were unpaid, and perhaps it is not surprising to learn that in 1740 it was found necessary to forbid the apparently established practice of entertaining friends at the parish expense on the occasion of diocesan visitations. By the 19th century, parish responsibilities had increased still further and the Vestry had expanded to include most of the gentry and leading tradesmen, though by 1820 the full body only met annually. Routine business was conducted by a Select Vestry composed of the elected officers and a representative body of the more influential parishioners who met every few weeks under the chairmanship of the vicar.

As well as constant maintenance of the roads and footpaths, and public works such as erecting a pump by the well at Pump Corner, there appears now to have been a greater emphasis on law and order. A new cage and a pair of handcuffs were provided, stocks were built on Butter Hill, and "three most stout and able Paupers" were employed to watch the streets. In census years, the parish officers had the added duty of organising the local enumerators and from 1832 the Overseers were responsible for compiling the electoral register. In this year too the Vestry arranged passages to Canada for emigrating Dorking families.

Church matters of course were still a major preoccupation, and many meetings were spent in discussing dilapidations and lack of seating, particularly for the poor. The problems were solved, temporarily at least, by the building of the Intermediate Church though this in itself caused even more work for the Vestry, and afterwards pew and gallery seats had to be leased out according to social status. This could lead to trouble as happened in 1837 when William Crawford of Pippbrook House went to the length of publishing a pamphlet to justify his claim to a front seat, on the grounds of the superiority of his house, and his position as a magistrate.

Responsibility for the Workhouse was transferred to a Board of Guardians in 1834, thus relieving the Vestry of one of their major burdens, but they must have welcomed the formation in 1881 of the Dorking Local Government Board, the forerunner of the District Council, leaving the clergy, churchwardens and parishioners once more to their traditional role of caring for the church and the needy until the creation in 1921 of a Parochial Church Council (PCC).

Charities

Before the Reformation ministering to the sick and needy was regarded as one of the prime duties of the church, and a proportion of its revenue was supposed to be devoted to this purpose. In addition, some at least of the men and women of Dorking belonged to a religious guild or brotherhood dedicated to the Blessed Mary which supported a priest to pray for the souls of its members, and very probably served as a mutual benefit society and social club as well. There is no record of the foundation of this brotherhood, but the altar in the north aisle of the church was dedicated to St. Mary, and it is tempting to connect this with the building additions of the 14th century, a period when many such guilds were formed in parishes all over the country. Certainly by 1385 the churchwardens were collecting overdue payment for a chaplain's salary from two of the local tradesmen, although it was not until a will of 1464 that the Brotherhood was mentioned by name. After this many wills contained bequests of cash or kind in its favour, and two Brotherhood priests, Thomas Grant and William Fox, figured both as beneficiaries and witnesses.

In 1548 religious guilds were dissolved, following the same fate as the monasteries, and eleven pieces of land, valued at an annual rent of 37s. 2d, which comprised the property of the Dorking Brotherhood, were bought by a local family. At the same time it was reported that there were 454 communicants within the parish, but it is not clear whether they all belonged to the guild. The altar in the south aisle dedicated to St. John could have been used by a second guild of which no record remains.

With the passing of all former ecclesiastical property into lay hands, the church no longer had the means to relieve the needy, and the gap was filled partly by the Poor Rate levied on all parishioners able to pay, and partly by the charity of individuals. In the Middle Ages, prayers for the dead were thought to be even more necessary than care for the living and much wealth was devoted to this end, but the practice was frowned on by the Church of England, and instead prosperous inhabitants bequeathed money or land for the benefit of the poor.

By the end of the 16th century the new owners of the Brotherhood lands had returned eight tenements on a piece of land in South Street to the churchwardens to be used as almshouses. These however must soon have become inadequate for the growing town, and in 1677, the Hon. Charles Howard of Deepdene and Sir Adam Browne of Betchworth, joint Lords of the Manor, granted part of Cotmandene for 2000 years at a peppercorn rent for building an establishment capable of accommodating eighteen inmates. The former site was developed as the first Workhouse and underwent a number of changes until the opening of the Union Workhouse in Horsham Road in 1841 made it redundant. In 1845 it was sold, together with property in Brockham and Betchworth, to finance the rebuilding of the Cotmandene almshouses. By a nice coincidence, in 1899 the original site in South Street, which then contained three cottages, a cab business, a coal and timber yard and a sweet shop, was acquired by the Methodists for their new church, which was built the following year.

Finance for the almshouses and for other charitable purposes came from various benefactors, prominent amongst whom was the celebrated Surrey philanthropist, Henry Smith of Wandsworth, a silversmith and Alderman of the City of London, who died in 1627. During his lifetime he gave £1,000 each to Dorking and four other towns in the county, to be invested in land to provide an income for the relief of the poor and setting them to work, and he also created a trust which after his death applied the bulk of his considerable fortune to similar purposes in nearly every Surrey parish. Dorking churchwardens invested his generous gift in land at Bottesford, Leicestershire, and parish property was further increased in 1661 by the bequest by the late vicar, Samuel Cozens, of an estate of 23 acres in Chislet, Kent, and again in 1718 when the executors of Mrs Susannah Smith endowed the new almshouses with the Duke's Head and other property in Brockham and Betchworth. In 1725 Mrs Margaret Fenwicke of Betchworth Castle left £800 for apprenticing poor children and giving dowries to deserving maid-servants, and this money was used to buy Fordland Farm in Albury.

At some date before 1649 an unknown benefactor left to 40 poor widows an annuity of 20 shillings arising from the rent of a field known as Poor Folk's Close which lay at the south east corner of St. Paul's and Horsham Roads. Also undated, but in effect by the mid-18th century, a distribution of penny loaves was made to the deserving poor every Good Friday at the parish church, and this was paid for out of the six shilling a year rent from a house in Brockham, the legacy of a William Hutton. Another bread dole, this time on New Year's Day, was that of Thomas Summers, a hatter of Horsham who travelled frequently to Dorking on business, and died in 1807 leaving £100 to be invested for this purpose.

Many legacies followed in the 19th century, generally in the form of income from investments in government stock, and they all had to be administered by the parish. Many of the original intentions, too, were no longer practical; even the poorest widow could hardly have been overjoyed by an annuity of sixpence in 1883. It must have been a great relief to the churchwardens when in that year the Charity Commissioners combined most of the charities into one fund, the Dorking Charities, to be administered by independent trustees and applied principally to supporting the almshouses and their inmates, and in apprenticing, leaving the residue for the sick and infirm poor. In today's welfare state the Trustees's sole care is the almshouses and all the land has been sold with the exception of Samuel Cozens's bequest at Chislet, now a very valuable property.

The Churchyard

It is often remarked that St. Martin's has quite a small churchyard for such a large and ancient parish, and a partial explanation was provided by excavations in 1989 in the former market area to the east of the present churchyard wall. These uncovered a row of graves dating from the 12th or 13th centuries and now outside the wall but lying several feet to the west of a ditch which could have formed an earlier boundary. The realignment may have occurred as the result of some official planning but there could be another answer. Although upkeep of the churchyard fell to the parish, each adjacent property owner was required by custom to maintain his individual length of boundary, and it is possible that one such medieval tenant succeeded in enlarging his property in the process. A similar contraction may have occurred on the southern boundary too, as it is claimed that at least two burials were exposed when Barclays Bank was being constructed in the 1960s.

There is no doubt that the churchyard was in use from at least the 13th century and early wills attest to regular burial there nearly a hundred years before the more complete records provided by the parish registers. During outbreaks of pestilence in the 16th and 17th centuries as many as 107 people were interred in one year and excepting the occasional emergency burial at home there is no indication that any special arrangements were made or that communal graves were resorted to. The rotation must therefore have been fairly rapid and the build-up so great that it was not surprising to find that by the time the medieval church was demolished, its floor, now in the crypt of the present church, had been left about six feet below the level of the churchyard.

The present gravestones which were recorded by the Dorking Local History Group in 1983 bear dates of no earlier than the 18th century, and this may correspond with the repairs to the gates, fences and paths in the churchyard ordered by the Vestry in 1762 after the removal of some walnut trees. Many of the parishioners who were buried previously must have had marked graves but these do not seem to have survived. The maintenance of the churchyard was a constant problem, and in the early 19th century the visiting Rural Dean complained that it was used as a drying ground and rubbish heap by the residents of adjoining properties. Apparently, too, at some date a privy had been installed within its confines; in 1816 when the Vestry was preparing to build the school it was proposed to demolish this structure which had "long been an offensive nuisance", but the proposal was thrown out.

The parish registers record that strangers occasionally found a last resting place alongside the parishioners of St. Martin's. Some were unknown, but during the Civil War a number of graves were allotted to soldiers who were billeted in the town and in the years when the Assizes were held in Dorking, the unfortunate men and women who were hanged for their crimes were buried within the churchyard. The problem of suicides and other excommunicates was solved in the usual compassionate fashion by allowing them technically unhallowed ground inside the north ditch.

Nonconformists were also buried in St. Martin's churchyard unless, like the Quakers, they had their own burial ground, and by 1855 it was full again. It was decided therefore to close it and to buy a large parcel of land along the Reigate Road for use as a town cemetery. Here an attractive group of flint buildings with tiled roofs was constructed. It included a cemetery church, caretaker's house and mortuary. From 22 February 1874, the cemetery church regularly had two services on Sundays at 11am and 3pm. When Pixham Church was opened in 1890 it seems clear that it was intended that the services there should be complementary to those at the cemetery. During the 1930s a children's service was held in the afternoon, and the cemetery church finally ceased to be used for Sunday services by July 1940.

Memorials and Monuments

There are records of burials inside the church from the 15th century onwards, though none was apparently marked until the very late 16th century when it became common practice for Dorking gentry to commemorate their dead with memorial tablets, generally placed in the floor of the nave or chancel, or on the walls of the latter, or in some equally prominent position. Two particularly ornate monuments, one to Catherine, the wife of Henry Talbot of Chart Park, who died in 1754, and the other to the Earl of Rothes, father of Lady Elizabeth Wathen of Shrub Hill, who died in 1817, flanked the screen bearing the figures of Moses and Aaron. Both of these survive in the tower, though that of Catherine Talbot is now incomplete.

Sadly, most of these memorials cannot now be traced. Some probably fell victim to the wholesale demolitions in the 19th century, but it is likely that many are now hidden from view under the modern chancel. It was fortunate therefore that various people, starting with John Aubrey in 1673, recorded in detail what they saw when they visited the church. From these descriptions it does not seem that St. Martin's ever had any outstanding tombs or brasses, although Aubrey says that a gravestone in the middle of the chancel in memory of William Adam of Saffron Walden, who was connected by marriage with the Brownes of Betchworth Castle, and who died in 1608, had lost its brass effigy of a gowned man.

Aubrey described thirteen tablets of brass or stone in his "Natural History and Antiquities of Surrey" and his editor Dr. Richard Rawlinson added another five before publishing the book in 1718. The same memorials were noted by Manning & Bray in their history published in 1805, with the addition of nine more recent ones, and during the 1974 excavations in the crypt two of the latter were discovered still in situ, inches deep in dust but exactly as described. A black marble tablet inscribed to John Hall and his wife lies in what would have been the south aisle, now partly covered by a piece of foundation wall from the Intermediate Church, and Mrs Sarah Courtenay's bricked grave lies next to the well, near the West end. E. W. Brayley also recorded what he saw in the Intermediate Church.

Most of the early 19th century memorials from the chancel listed in the faculty of 1866 were discovered in the crypt by Mr. G. Gardiner when he was a churchwarden in 1899 and re-erected in the tower. It was, however, considered appropriate to place the tablet to Mrs. Margaret Fenwicke in the Almshouses, (now on the outside back wall), as a reminder of their indebtedness to her.

The Changing Life of the Parish

The destruction of the medieval church during the middle decades of the 19th century and its eventual replacement by the modern St. Martin's was only one event in a period of rapid change which affected nearly every aspect of parish life. The creation of new parishes, the purchase of a new vicarage, the opening of the cemetery, the establishment of St. Martin's school, the formation of local authorities to relieve the Vestry of its burden of civic duties; all these were matched by new thinking amongst churchmen and a resurgence of community life centred on the church.

Chapter 3

The Intermediate and Present Churches

The Intermediate Church

From the beginning of the 19th century there were persistent claims that the parish church was inadequate, both as to its size and its condition. These came to a head at a Special Vestry meeting on 6 January 1829, and on the next day a printed notice was addressed to all parishioners stating 'that from the delapidated state of the Church, and from the want of accommodation for numerous Parishioners desirous of attending divine worship therein, it is highly expedient that the Church should be either repaired and enlarged, or rebuilt.' A public subscription was proposed, but the proposal fell on stony ground. Since 1800 the vicar had been George Feachem. It seems likely that towards the end of his life he was often ill. The matter was allowed to rest.

It was in 1835, with the arrival of a new curate, Stephen Isaacson, that plans finally materialised, and then very fast. After the first meeting, on 9 May 1835, where it was agreed to rebuild the nave, with the expected cost of £4,000 coming from public subscriptions, he was always in the chair of the Dorking Church Building Committee. The committee decided to choose the architect by way of a competition, at that date still quite a novel procedure. The advertisement to architects and surveyors, which survives, invited designs to be submitted anonymously. The project was to take down the nave and rebuild it so that it would contain 1,800 sittings, of which one third were to be free. The floor of the nave was to be raised about seven feet and the plan was to allow communion to take place 'in the Body of the Church'. 'The arrangements of the underpart of the new Church are to be so made as to facilitate the formation of Burial Vaults'. This was an ingenious idea which would both solve the difficulty that the floor of the medieval nave was then considerably lower than the surrounding churchyard, and the fact that the churchyard was almost full once more. Again, it is tempting to ascribe this proposal to the eager young curate. The prizes offered were small, £30 for the first prize and £15 for the second, and the time allowed for the competition, four weeks, very short. Both these conditions may have militated against the quality of the designs sent in.

By 10 June 1835 Mr. Hart, the Vestry Clerk, reported that twenty plans had been received. There were eventually to be twenty-three. The meeting of 12 June then selected plan no: 1, with the pseudonym 'Cantab'. This was discovered to be the work of the London architect William McIntosh Brookes. It is not known when he was born but he studied with George Maddox (1760-1843) who was celebrated as an architectural drawing-master, and whose most famous pupils were the neo-classical designer, Decimus Burton, and the great gothic revivalist, George Gilbert Scott. Brookes designed both neo-classical and gothic buildings, and at the time of the Dorking competition his major work was the dull Tudor gothic Gisborne Court at Peterhouse College, Cambridge, which was built between 1825 and 1826. He was later to design several buildings in Surrey, notably the Catholic Apostolic church and the new parish church, both at Albury. He died in 1849.

The design which won second prize, by James Harrison, of 7 Amwell Terrace, Claremont Square, London, survives in the Dorking Museum and shows interesting similarities to that of Brookes. A huge rectangular preaching-box with extensive galleries and simple gothic detail was being provided. An avant-garde feature of Brookes' design, however, was that the pillars in the nave were made of cast-iron. This material had been used as beams in industrial buildings since the end of the eighteenth century. Thomas Rickman had pioneered its use in Liverpool churches in the second decade of the 19th century, and Nash used it for columns and staircases at the Royal Pavilion, Brighton, at the same period, but it was still a most unusual choice.

It is tempting to think that the Church Building Committee was not considering the design, but merely the space provided, and concentrated on raising the funds as soon as possible. Several large donations were made by the major local landowners. By 24 June when nearly £4,500 had been raised the Committee announced that it 'would not do Justice to their Feelings were they not to make known to you the high gratification they have felt in observing the general spirit which has manifested itself among the young — the Domestics and the Poor who have equally sought to contribute their willing gifts, thus proving how acceptable a Work the Committee have in hand'. The new nave was to cost £4,000, but repairs to the chancel, transepts and spire would add a further £1,500 to £1,800.

All must have seemed well, however, when a grand procession watched by an estimated 10,000 people, formed up in the town on 28 October 1835, 'a particularly fine day', according to a surviving annotated programme, to see Dr. Sumner, Bishop of Winchester, lay the foundation stone. Dorking must have seemed a very progressive place, and the work got under way swiftly with Samuel Bothwell, a local man, as contractor. Taking down the nave, however, must have disturbed the central tower, which then became unsafe, and on 21 May 1836 it was reported that it was necessary to take down the north transept and rebuild it. Throughout this year there were constant complaints from the contractor that the architect would not let him have the drawings that were needed for the work. On 10 September 1836 the vicar applied to the Incorporated Church Building Society for a grant saying that because it had been found necessary to rebuild the central tower and both transepts, expenses had been greater than expected. The work had already been done, and the plan submitted with the application, both of which survive in Lambeth Palace Library, shows massive strengthening to the tower, which had been raised and was now surmounted by an octagonal spire. The plan also shows that the south transept became the main porch, with staircases to the galleries, and a robing room beyond to the south-east beside the medieval chancel. The north transept, though rebuilt, kept its unusual medieval elevation and became the vestry room with a separate north-eastern entrance.

On 27 December 1836 the architect presented his report and account, totalling £6,999. It seems that the building was substantially completed by that time and early the following year fittings were being purchased for the new building. The pulpit which, together with the reading desk, must have dominated the east end of the nave, was found by the assiduous Mr. Isaacson, and agreed to on 16 March 1837. On 18 July 1837 a similar procession formed up, when the Bishop of Winchester again came to Dorking, to consecrate the new church. George Feachem had died in office on 7 February 1837 and James Joyce had become vicar.

Unexecuted competition drawing for the Intermediate Church, longitudinal section through the new nave, showing proposed burial vaults below the floor, the medieval central tower and chancel, a watercolour of 1835 by James Harrison who won second prize.

South-east view of the Intermediate Church, showing the new nave, the rebuilt central tower and spire and medieval chancel, a lithograph of c1855.

The nave of the Intermediate Church looking west, with the organ at the west end, and the present pulpit to the right, an engraving of 1839.

View of the interior of the medieval chancel looking east, an engraving of 1839.

Designs for the chancel presented to the donor, W. H. Forman, watercolours by the architect, Henry Woodyer, 1866.

South-east view of the exterior of the Forman Chancel, a photograph taken c1870.

The stained glass of 1867 by William Wailes in the east window of the chancel.

The important matter of the pews, which were allocated in accordance with the sums subscribed, then had to be dealt with, and produced some local annoyance. The fact that the church had cost considerably more than expected did not surface until January 1838 when the contractor was asking for settlement on unpaid bills. Agreed accounts were finally presented on 2 June 1838, which showed that expenses were £8,917 5s 0d, and that £6,878 had been raised, leaving a deficit of £2,039. It is interesting to note that Mr. Joyce had taken over as Chairman of the Building Committee, and Mr. Isaacson left Dorking in 1838. Various strategies were tried to overcome the deficit: further requests were made for subscriptions, counsel's opinion was taken about the legality of raising a rate retrospectively on work already done, and finally a loan was advanced. It was not until 24 January 1840 that the financial situation was finally resolved and the committee wound up.

If the Intermediate Church had survived, it would have been a remarkable and rare example of its period, but never a lovely one.

The Present Church: the Forman Chancel

The Intermediate Church lapped around the medieval chancel, making it almost invisible from the outside. A new small chancel was formed under the tower, separated by a flight of steps from the old one. According to E. W. Brayley, it 'is still occasionally used for prayers and christenings'. W. H. Forman, following the death of Hannah Moore, who was buried in the Forman chapel in St. George's church, Doncaster, in 1866, offered to rebuild the chancel. (*See* Chapter 4). A faculty was granted for this purpose, stating that the cost would be £3,700.

It is most interesting to speculate on Mr. Forman's choice of architect for the work, Henry Woodyer. Both his previous building exploits, at the church at Doncaster, and at his own house in Dorking, Pippbrook, had been in the hands of George Gilbert Scott, who was at the height of his career, and had just built the fine local church of St. Barnabas, Ranmore. Perhaps Pippbrook, certainly one of Scott's duller works, did not please him completely. It would be very nice to know what influenced him to turn to Woodyer, who undoubtedly did have a good reputation at that date. It should be remembered that Woodyer had built the church and college of St. Michael, Tenbury, for the Revd. Sir Frederick Gore Ouseley, who was a close friend of the then vicar of St. Martin's, W. H. Joyce. Did Mr. Forman take Sir Frederick's advice?

Woodyer was born in 1816 and was pupil of the great mid-Victorian church architect, William Butterfield. Like Butterfield, Woodyer specialised in churches, and from 1860 he was living at and working from Grafham in Surrey. He had built good new churches at Grafham and Hascombe in Surrey, Higham in Gloucestershire and Wokingham in Berkshire, before he began at Dorking. Here he took as his starting point the spendid 14th century east window, and he designed his chancel in a grand Decorated style, using the local knapped flint as his building material. The original drawings remained with the Forman family until recently, when they were bought by Surrey Record Office. The eastward extensions of the Intermediate Church were removed and the result looked impresssive from the outside. The consecration service took place on 30 April 1868.

Forman not only built the chancel but also decorated it sumptuously. These furnishings are discussed below but the chancel screen, because it has been removed, is mentioned here. Such a screen in the mid-19th century was almost a symbol of High Church, Tractarian views, and it is interesting to read in Miss Mayo's account, *Concerning the Three Churches in Dorking Dedicated to St Martin*, that W. H. Joyce wanted one. She gave it in 1870 and it was put in place shortly after Joyce's death, with a brass plate to his memory.

The Rebuilding of the 1870s

It seems that the Intermediate Church had never been greatly admired. Brayley in his *History of Surrey* says that it 'has little to recommend it in respect to architectural beauty'. The Rural Dean in 1852 considered that the rebuilding was in 'bad taste'. Obviously opinions about architectural style changed rapidly in the middle of the 19th century; in 1837 the gothic revival had hardly begun its serious antiquarian phase, by 1870 nothing else was possible. Once the new chancel was built, fitted up and in use, the liturgical arrangement of the building must have been very strange, with most of the service taking place out of sight beyond the constricted central tower. And yet to knock down the nave, within the living memory of many who had subscribed to it and remembered the subsequent wrangles over paying for it, was surely an extraordinary decision.

Yet it was taken by the vicar who succeeded W. H. Joyce, Philip Hoste. The leading lay member behind the scheme seems to have been Arthur Powell (1812-94), who was senior partner in the glassmaking firm of James Powell & Sons of Whitefriars. This firm from 1844 had a department for making stained glass, which by 1871 had become one of the most important and progressive in the country. According to Stiff, Arthur Powell moved to Dorking from Clapton in 1858, and lived at Milton Heath. While in London he had been prominent in a movement of church revival which Stiff calls 'the Hackney Phalanx or the Clapton Sect', and had helped provide new churches in Clapton and Dalston. It was inevitable that, in aesthetic terms, he would look on the Intermediate Church with horror.

The project got under way in 1871, the year in which Powell was churchwarden. On 22 April it was resolved to appoint Woodyer for proposed alterations and additions to the church and on 26 June he submitted plans. Given the coherence of the plan of the church as it now is, it seems almost inconceivable that Woodyer had not designed a complete church when he had made his designs for the chancel in 1866. There is, however, no evidence for this. On 4 January 1872 the church received a faculty to pull down the nave, and Woodyer was asked to get tenders for the work. Here it is obvious that there was a much more cautious approach than last time, and a determination only to do work that could be paid for. At this date also there was much tighter control over builders. The tenders were all too high, and the architect was asked to scale down the plan. It is not known, however, what he omitted as a result of this request, but his design continues the scale and style of his earlier chancel, and culminates with a very grand west tower and spire. In May £4,620 had been raised and the builders, Goddard & Sons, had tendered £5,491. On 15 July there was a public luncheon given by the Restoration Committee, at which the Bishop of Winchester, Dr. Wilberforce, Mr. Cubitt and Mr. Powell all spoke, and £263 was collected. The contract was signed and in August the demolition work began. Building proceeded rapidly.

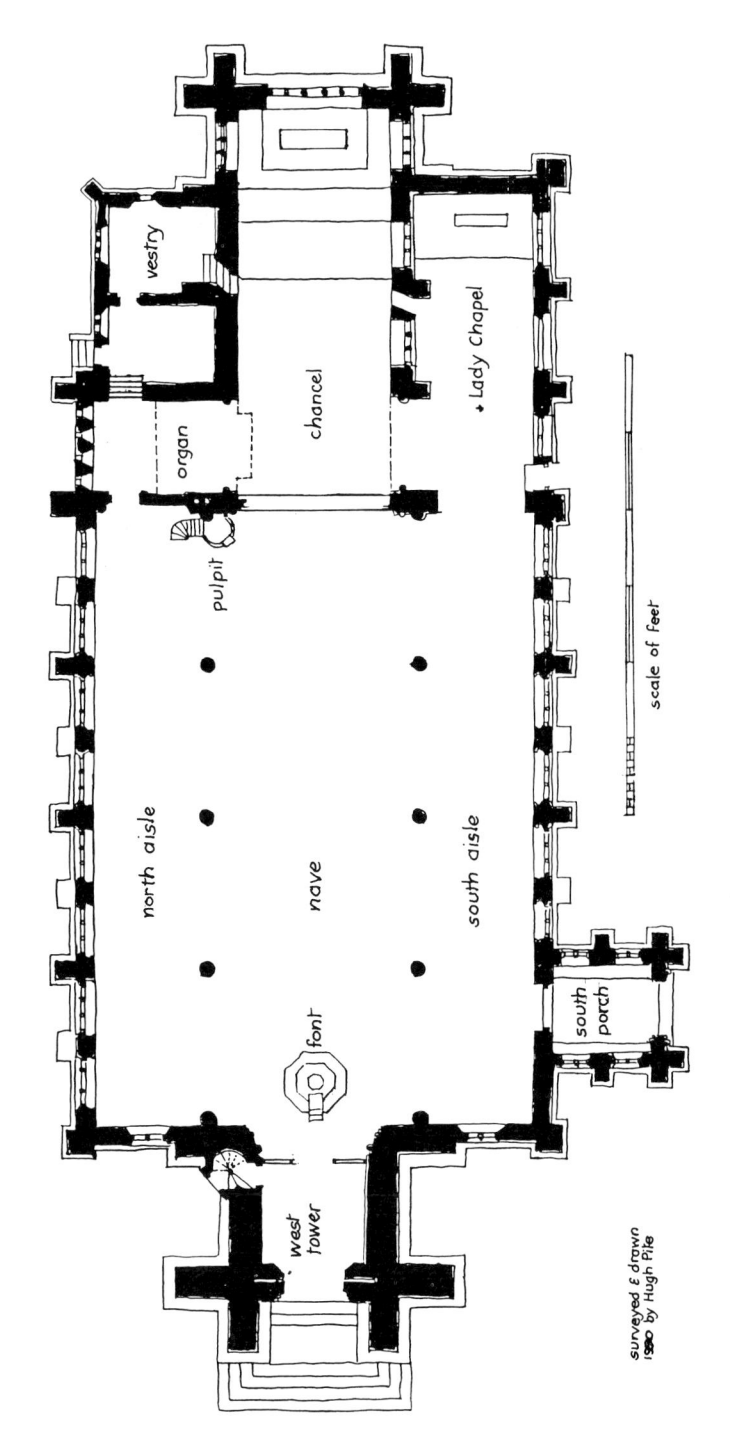

PLAN of CHURCH of St. MARTIN

surveyed & drawn
1980 by Hugh Pike

South-east view of the church, a photograph taken in 1978.

On 29 May 1873 Dr. Wilberforce was back in Dorking to lay the foundation stone of the tower. On 19 July the Bishop was killed by a fall from his horse, the same day the Restoration Committee recorded that subscriptions of £5,199 10s 7d had been received and payments made of £5,122 14s 4d. The money was coming in slowly and mostly in quite small sums. As a fund-raising idea, it was decided to build the tower and spire as a 'Wilberforce Memorial'.

The church was reopened on 11 June 1874, St. Barnabas's Day, when 30 clergy were present, the choir was augmented by a contingent from St. Mark's, Reigate, and the new Bishop of Winchester, Dr. Browne, preached. There was still much to do, and from 1875 a new vicar, the Revd. Peter Righton Atkinson, was in charge. In 1876 the south porch and vestries were built. But it was the tower and the spire which presented the greatest challenge. In order to encourage funds, an appeal was made to restore 'to the Town its well known and beautiful Bells'. Finally on 25 April 1877 the top stone of the spire was laid. The height to the top of the weathervane is 210 feet. The bells were rehung at the expense of Mrs. Burt and first rang again on 21 December 1877. In the Parish Magazine for 1879 appeals were made to settle the final accounts on the building. One can only admire the tenacity with which this great project was carried through! And having built the church, the congregation over the next 50 years put much effort into decorating it. This work is described below.

20th Century Additions and Alterations

The cruciform shape of the old medieval church survived in Woodyer's building with north and south transepts, the northern one forming part of the vestries. In 1905 the south transept was made into the Lady Chapel and between 1912 and 1913 this was extended under the direction of the architect Basil Champneys (1842-1935) in commemoration of Canon Chichester's silver jubilee as vicar. It makes an effective composition from the outside and, like all the other additions, looks as if it was part of the original design. That it is not, is obvious from the inside, where it encloses two stained glass windows in the south wall of the chancel. Basil Champneys also designed the War Memorial in the churchyard.

No further changes took place until the 1960s. The liturgical movement of that period sought to bring the celebration of the eucharist closer to the people, with centrally placed altars and the priest facing the people. At St. Martin's the long chancel, and in particular the chancel screen, were thought to be a disadvantage. (There are odd reminders of the Intermediate Church in some of the arguments!) Some radical schemes were proposed by the church architect, Jim Ralph, but the agreed scheme of 1965 was quite conservative, concentrating on redecoration, heating and lighting. The chancel screen was, however, removed.

Church Halls and the Christian Centre

The church halls are situated to the west of the church, on a site which was originally part of Cape Place. It was bought in 1878 by Mr. George Cubitt and most of the money for the new building was given by Mrs. Hope of the Deepdene. This hall, known as the 'Church Room' and built of flint in keeping with the church, was opened on 24 February

1879. It was designed by Mr. Rhode Hawkins. Later that year the parish opened St. Martin's Coffee Room and Invalid Kitchen further to the north on the same site, adjoining the verger's cottage.

The Church Room was used chiefly by the women and in 1900 a 'munificent and anonymous friend' provided for the building of a large room adjoining the Church Room to be a 'Club Room for our Young Men', which was equipped with billiard and bagatelle tables. The Club Room, Coffee Room and verger's cottage were all rebuilt in the early 1920s when the Revd. Thomas Hayter was vicar, and for about 50 years there were no more major changes. Then with the decision by the Anglicans and the Methodists to join together in a Shared Church came also the decision to rebuild the halls as the Christian Centre. The architect chosen was Robert Potter and between 1976 and 1977 he provided for the retention and modernisation of the old flint hall and the small rooms and kitchen behind, and the addition of an entirely new two-storied block over the remainder of the site. On the entrance facade to the churchyard, his three new gabled bays, with their big aluminium-framed windows of frosted glass set in concrete, are a sensitive complement in both colour and proportion to the earlier building with its three big mullioned and transomed windows (*see* also Chapters 6 and 7).

The Furnishings

The only survivals from the medieval church apart from the bells are some monuments most of which are now in the tower. Two of them record particularly eminent 18th century parishioners, both of whom were writers. There is a brass plate with a splendid inscription on the west wall of the north aisle to Jeremiah Markland (1693-1776), the classical scholar and critic, who lived for many years at Milton Court, and a handsome mural monument in the tower to Abraham Tucker (1705-1774) of Betchworth Castle, who has been described as a 'philosophical humourist' (*DNB*). The survivals from the Intermediate Church include some more monuments and the late gothic Netherlandish pulpit. This is a handsome wooden octagonal one on a tall stem. It has a panel containing a carving of St. Martin sharing his cloak with the beggar, and there are other little statues of saints standing on columns. It came from the Bond Street shop of John Webb, who by 1837 was one of the leading antique dealers in the country and may have restored it. It was reduced in height when the nave was rebuilt in the 1870s.

The main furnishings, of course, date from the building of the present church and can be conveniently divided into two distinct groups, those in the Forman chancel and those dominated by the work of James Powell & Sons of Whitefriars. The chancel was presented by W. H. Forman as an entity, completely fitted out. The reredos, altar, crucifix, seven sanctuary lamps, altar candlesticks and the two great standing candlesticks were all given at this time. The reredos has a central panel of English alabaster, into which are placed a gilt brass crucifix and the symbols of the four evangelists carved in stone. To either side are carved stone panels, one with figures of angels, the other with saints, led by King Edward the Confessor and St. Alban. All the brasswork was made by the firm of John Hardman of Birmingham, a major supplier of such items in the gothic revival style in the second half of the 19th century.

The major decorative feature of the chancel, however, is the stained glass, which was

View of the interior of the church looking east, showing the first Lady Chapel as it existed between 1905 and 1912, the chancel screen of 1870, and early examples of electric lights, a photograph taken c1912.

A window in the south aisle showing Christ blessing the children, *A window in the north aisle showing the story of Noah, 1894.*
1888.

Stained glass by James Powell & Sons.

made by William Wailes of Newcastle, who was one of the important manufacturers of the middle years of the 19th century. It has been discovered that similar glass, also by Wailes, clearly using some of the same cartoons, was used a few years earlier in the chapel at St. George's church, Doncaster, which W. H. Forman also paid for. The four windows with standing figures of the Apostles above scenes from the Acts of the Apostles are identical in both places. Both east windows have scenes from the Resurrection, but at St. Martin's, where the window is much larger, there are also scenes from the Passion. At St. Martin's there are also two completely new windows, those at the north-east and south-east ends of the chancel, showing the life of St. Martin of Tours. The bright colours and medieval figures and architectural details in these windows are typical of the decorative work of the middle years of the century.

In the rest of the church after 1875, however, there is a very different style and the guiding hand of Arthur Powell in the decoration of the then empty church is obvious. He does not seem to have had any control over the first window of the new building, which was that in what was then the south transept. This window, with the subject of the Transfiguration treated in a conventional manner, was given in 1874 to the memory of James Joyce and his wife Sarah by their youngest daughter Laura Cubitt, but subsequently altered (see below). But the following year the windows in memory of W. H. Joyce show the start of the work by Powell and the pattern that was largely followed in the rest of the work.

These windows are the most eastern one in the south aisle and the most eastern pair in the south clerestory. In the firm's order books it is recorded that these cost £90 and £50 respectively and were designed by Harry Burrow. He had joined Powell & Son in 1872 and was influenced by their chief designer, Henry Holiday (1839-1927). The style, which may be called 'the Aesthetic Movement', is in great contrast to the earlier work in the chancel. Here there are large clear figures, classical draperies, cool colours and much naturalistic detail of fruit and foliage. It is also the start of a programme of iconography, with the theme of each window explained to the congregation on a brass plate, clearly legible. The window in the south aisle is labelled 'Christ teaching by Suffering', and shows the Ecce Homo, Betrayal and Agony in the Garden. Following an old tradition, all the subjects in the south aisle are from the New Testament, those in the north from the Old Testament.

It was then a few more years before any more windows were put in the church, though Arthur Powell himself put simple glass in the porch in 1876 and a window in the church hall in 1879, which was removed as being unsafe in 1976. In 1883 the next window in the south aisle and those in the clerestory above, all following the established pattern, were given in memory of P. L. Saubergue. The aisle window illustrates 'Christ teaching by Miracles', with Christ stilling the waters, raising Lazarus and healing the blind. In 1884 windows of the Annunciation and the Adoration of the Shepherds were placed respectively at the west ends of the north and south aisles and decorative glass in the west wall of the tower, in memory of J. E. Bovill. These were from cartoons supplied by Henry Holiday, as was the next window to be supplied, that at the west end of the south aisle. This was given by Archdeacon Atkinson in the year he left Dorking. It is labelled 'Lessons of Holy Childhood' and shows Christ and the Doctors and the Flight into Egypt. The cartoons for these windows cost £70 and had first been made, according to Powell's window glass order book, for a church in Albany, New York State.

A window to commemorate Queen Victoria's Golden Jubilee in 1887 illustrated Christ teaching by Parable, and shows the Angel Reaper, the Good Shepherd and Christ the Sower. The cost of £90 was raised by public subscription, and the order book says that the figures of the Shepherd and the Sower are from new cartoons by Brown. He was J. W. Brown (1842-1928) who had come to Powell's as a key designer in 1877 and designed most of the remaining windows in the church, and perhaps some of the mosaics. His masterpiece is the east window of Liverpool Anglican cathedral. The missing gaps in the south aisle and in the clerestory above were then quickly filled in 1888 by a window in memory of J. W. Joyce showing the Sermon on the Mount, and one in memory of Archdeacon Atkinson showing Christ blessing children. Some of the figures in the clerestory windows were designed by George Parlby, who was a colleague of J. W. Brown.

The first window to go in the north aisle, a particularly fine one by Brown costing £100, shows the Fall, with the Temptation, the Angel of the Lord, and the Expulsion. As with the other windows on the north aisle, the drawing is less conventional and the design less cluttered than those on the south aisle. The brass plate states 'To the Glory of God and as a Thankoffering for many mercies vouchsafed, a parishioner of Dorking, who a few years back was permitted to take part in the rebuilding of this church, now presents the above window AD 1889'. The order book identifies the parishioner as Arthur Powell himself.

Some items other than windows were also added at this time, notably the wooden screen under the tower arch, given in 1886 in memory of J. G. Stilwell, and the octagonal font, which looks like a grander version of the one in the Intermediate Church, given in 1897 in memory of John Edward and Priestly Mary Bovill.

The Powell firm did not specialise only in stained glass; they also made a form of mural decoration known as *opus sectile*, which has been described as standing halfway between tile painting and stained glass. Slabs of opaque glass are painted with enamel colour and fired. The pieces are fixed to the wall by cement and the designs are usually surrounded by a frame of canopy work in marble or alabaster, with sometimes a little added mosaic in gold or colour. The great work in this medium at St. Martin's is the decoration over the chancel arch. The central panel with the crucifixion was in place by 1892 and according to the Parish Magazine was the gift of 'a parishioner'. The firm's order book does not give the identity of the donor, but does mention that the design is by G. W. Rhead. This must be George Woolliscroft Rhead Jr. (1855-1920). The son of G. W. Rhead (1832-1908), he was an artist and ceramic designer, who also wrote about design. In 1901 the decoration in the remainder of the chancel arch, still apparently to the designs of G. W. Rhead, was completed as a memorial to Queen Victoria. It was dedicated on 23 March 1902 by the vicar. When one admires its satisfying composition and colours, it is worth remembering the great effort that went into raising the necessary money, about £350. There were several appeals in the Parish Magazine for funds to pay for it, and Powells waived one quarter of their price.

In 1894 Arthur Powell died, and, as a tribute to his outstanding contribution to the rebuilding and decoration of the church, several more windows were added, as a result

Wall monument to Henry Harman Young (1895-1915) in the north aisle.

Wall panel of 1898 in the south aisle commemorating Queen Victoria's Diamond Jubilee.

Work in *opus sectile* by James Powell & Sons.

Carved reredos in the Lady Chapel, showing the Crucifixion, designed by G. F. Bodley in 1904.

of a public subscription. These were the remaining clerestory windows on the south side, the first ones on the north side and the second north aisle window, which illustrates the history of Noah and the Flood. Powell's memorial from his family is a wall monument in *opus sectile* between the first two windows of the north aisle. It shows the Angel's message to Hagar. Two very similar panels were put up in the south aisle to commemorate Queen Victoria's Diamond Jubilee of 1897.

Even without Powell's presence, his firm continued to dominate all decorative work carried out within the church. It should be remembered that Arthur Powell's eldest son, Arthur Crofts Powell, who was also a partner in the family business, continued to live in Dorking, first at Townfield and then at Bencomb. Canon Chichester seems to have appreciated the firm's work, and used the Powell firm almost exclusively throughout his vicariate. Two more windows were added in the north aisle, one in 1904 of the Patriachs, showing Isaac, Jacob and Joseph, in memory of Frederick Flood, the brother of a former curate, and the other in 1908 with the history of Moses, in memory of John and Caroline Young.

Meanwhile, the south transept was transformed between 1904 and 1905 into the Lady Chapel. The central feature here was the very fine altarpiece with the crucified Christ between the Virgin and St. John. It was given in memory of Mrs Symonds, and was one of the last works of one of the most sensitive gothic revival designers of the late 19th century, G. F. Bodley (1827-1907). There followed in 1905 the *opus sectile* memorial to Lady Ashcombe, the daughter of James Joyce and the mother of Mrs Chichester, who had died in 1904. This was placed at the east end, to either side of the altarpiece, and uses much gold mosaic in the background. Between 1912 and 1913 this chapel was extended in memory of Canon Chichester's silver jubilee in the parish, as has already been mentioned. This must have entailed moving the memorial to Lady Ashcombe, as well as the altarpiece. The marble slabs on the wall of the earlier chapel were also repeated in the extension. The site of the altar in the earlier chapel is marked by a cross in the floor, paid for by the Sunday School children, who each contributed a penny. Glass was put in the two new windows; in 1913 Powells designed the south-east window with subjects connected with the Virgin Mary, which was given in memory of F. Taylor, and in 1915 they altered the first window of the new church, given in 1874 and then in the south transept, so that it matched the new scheme. The middle window, which was put up in memory of Edward Arnold, appears not to be by Powell. It illustrates saints and prophets, with biblical scenes in roundels, and on the grounds of style may be attributed to the workshop of C. E. Kempe.

There was further work in *opus sectile* by the Powells in the Lady Chapel. The order book records the design for the Flight into Egypt by Coakes, which was ordered by Mrs Addis in 1914. Probably the companion panel of the Adoration of the Magi is of the same date. Several alterations and additions are noted to the panels at the east end, some in 1914, the Christ in Glory in 1918 above the altarpiece, and a final addition in 1921. The Lady Chapel had almost become the 'Chichester Chapel', and here are the two memorials to the Canon's son, W. G. C. Chichester (1892-1916), who was killed in the First World War. One of these monuments shows a knight kneeling before Christ. Another war memorial, showing a youthful St. George, was placed in the north aisle memory of Henry Harman Young (1894-1915).

Two fine monuments of very different character conclude the list of notable furnishings of the church. That beside the south porch to Lily, Duchess of Marlborough, was 'erected by friends and parishioners of Dorking' in 1910 to a design by Coakes in *opus sectile*, according to the Powell order book, and, outside in the south porch, a low relief bronze plaque in memory of Dr Ralph Vaughan Williams (1872-1958) was set up in 1961. It was made by the sculptor David McFall (born 1919). There is a duplicate in the foyer of the Dorking Halls. The most recent stained glass to be put in the church is that in the north-west corner of the north aisle, in the area made into the Children's Corner by G. Haynes, and dedicated on 24 February 1946. The windows are in memory of Mr and Mrs John C. H. Barnes.

Vestments, Frontals and Kneelers

The sequence of colours prescribed for the seasons of the ecclestastical year is *white* for Christmas and Easter, and *red* for Whitsun, *green* for Trinity and *purple* for Advent.

During the building of the Forman chancel Miss Mary Mayo organised the making of four altar cloths or frontals, each in one of these "liturgical" colours, and presented them at the consecration ceremony in 1868. Originally every frontal had a matching set of chasuble, pair of stoles, burse and veil, but not all have survived. From the concluding paragraph in Miss Mayo's book, *Pixham 1862-1912*, we know that she gave the white, green and purple frontals and her friend, Miss Noble, gave the red one.

In style the designs are typically High Victorian, formal, symmetrical and dignified. Each is divided into three compartments outlined with repeating border patterns, and enclosing a single symbol — the sacred monogram IHS, wheat, grapes, fleur de lys, etc. Miss Noble's, by contrast, has identical stars entwined with passion flowers and tendrils.

The embroidery is impeccable and is executed chiefly in long and short stitch and couching, with floss and twisted silks. Following the practice of the period the designs are outlined in stem stitch in shades ranging from light silvery grey to dark brown. With some pride Miss Mayo observed, "A great deal of my work is in all of them. All the rest was done by the Sisters at Wantage," i.e. by the Community of St Mary the Virgin whose well known School of Embroidery at Wantage (Berks) was much favoured by leading architects.

Miss Mayo herself worked the whole of the central panel on the white frontal. "It represents," she wrote, "the Lamb that had been slain standing on the Mount with the four rivers flowing from it. The blue background is solid needlework, and, with the border framing it, the whole took me more than a year to do. The Altar cloth was designed by Mr Preedy." (See *Frederick Preedy. Architect and Glass painter 1820-98*, Gordon Barnes FSA, 1984).

In 1969 the Overton family presented a Festal frontal *en suite* with a set of vestments, burse and veil, designed and worked by Beryl Dean. In the hundred years that separate the Forman and Overton frontals ideas on church needlework have changed radically; embroiderers have become their own designers, and it is now desirable that the design on a frontal should be clearly seen from the back of the church. Miss Mayo's frontals by contrast, are in scale with the patterned stonework behind and around the altar.

So Beryl Dean could write in her book *Ecclesiastical Embroidery* (Batsford 1958): "There

Central panel of the white altar frontal, which was designed by F. Preedy and worked by Mary Mayo, who gave it to St. Martin's in 1868.

Detail from the gold and white festival frontal, which was designed by Beryl Dean, and given to St. Martin's, together with a matching set of vestments, by the Overton family in 1969.

Bells nos. 2, 3, 4 and 5 in the 'up' position, ready to ring, a photograph taken in 1990.

Mr. Dodd, the verger, standing between Miss Cottrell and Miss Adams, with other lady bell ringers, a photograph taken c1915.

is no valid reason for limiting the decoration on a frontal to a series of divided panels . . . or one large central motif." Accordingly her design is an imaginative, asymmetrical composition of radiating stars of different magnitude, executed with great technical expertise in applied gold kid, laid gold threads and cords, beads and sequins on a white woollen crepe background.

The Lady Chapel has a charming little frontal woven in one piece, with an integral superfrontal, in a brocade weave with a gold thread ground. It is probably French and may have formed part of the collection of embroideries presented by Lily, Duchess of Marlborough, in memory of her husband who had died at the end of 1900. The design consists of a wreath of roses, convolvulus and leafy sprays surrounding a circle of cherub heads.

The kneelers in the Lady Chapel were worked in memory of Dr Ralph Vaughan Williams in 1972. His house in Dorking is featured on one of them, and others celebrate his musical compositions — London Symphony, Lark Ascending, etc.

When the Dorking Branch of the Embroiderers' Guild celebrated its 10th anniversary in 1985 a group of members designed and presented two marriage kneelers, in colours chosen to tone with the furnishings in the Forman chancel.

From time to time groups of needlewomen have come together to mend the frontals and vestments and renew the altar linen. The earliest reference to such a society occurs in the *Activities* listed in the Parish Magazine for May 1889. It reads: "The Needlework Society meets in the Church Room every Monday at 11 am"; but after the issue for the following November, no more is heard of it.

In the same year there was evidently a movement towards the replacement of an old banner, and the September issue has this: "We possess a Banner, but it is generally admitted to be quite unworthy of the Parish Church". In response to this the matter came up before the Annual General Meeting of the Guild of St Martin, reported in the December issue which reads: "It was decided to give £5 as a nucleus for a fund to provide a new Banner for the Church." Unfortunately there is no surviving reference to its commissioning and dedication.

The Organ

At a special Vestry meeting called in January 1831 a hearty vote of thanks was accorded to the churchwardens, Messrs James Cheeseman and Richard Attlee, who had been instrumental in raising the money for the purchase of an organ.

The instrument was constructed by Messrs Elliott and Hill and erected on a gallery above the chancel arch of the medieval church. When the Intermediate Church was erected the organ, having been dismantled and put into store, was rebuilt in 1837 in the gallery at the west end without any apparent tonal alterations. There appear to be two different versions of the tonal scheme available, but the one printed in E. W. Brayley, *History of Surrey*, V, [1848], is more historically correct compared with other instruments of that period.

Brayley gives the stops as follows: 'in the Great organ, two open diapasons, stop diapason, principal, twelfth, fifteenth, cornet, sesquialtra, mixture, trumpet. Choir organ, stop diapason, dulciana, principal, flute, cremona. Swell organ, two diapasons, principal, trumpet, hautboy; with an octave and half of open diapason pedals'. From the pipework in the Swell organ it is evident that the compass was from Tenor C upwards.

The order book of J. W. Walker gives us a clear picture of the rebuilding of the organ when the medieval chancel was replaced by the present edifice in 1868. Plans of the chancel recently purchased by the Surrey Record Office show quite clearly the new position of the organ in the north archway of the old central tower projecting into the north transept. From these plans one can only presume that the egress of sound into the nave was very restricted. The following is the entry in Walker's order book dated February 1868 as transcribed by John Horley:

The Organ in Dorking Church entirely reconstructed to suit new position made of the C C Compass and enlarged as follows:
Making New Swell Organ Wind Chest of 8 stops and New Swell Compass C C to F in Alto 54 notes, using the former pipes as far as available - adding a Double Diapason Stop 54 pipes 16ft tone. Adding a Mixture Stop 2 ranks 12th and 15th. New Cornopean Stop inserted in place of Trumpet, and new Oboe in place of former stop, both being inefficient . . .

The Great Organ Mixtures rearranged as this:-
Full mixture 2 Ranks   (1st CC to Mid. C 19th Mid C♯ to top 12th
                         (2nd   to   22nd   to top 15th
Sharp Mixture 2 Ranks (1st CC to Mid. C 26th Mid C♯ to Treb. G 19th Treb. G♯
                         (2nd   to   29th   to top - Principal
                         Mid C♯ to Treb. G 22nd Treb. G♯ to top - 15th

Tierce stop placed on separate slide to be used by itself if required. Inserting a Piccolo stop in Choir Organ CC to F - 54 notes 2ft with action and necessary enlargement of wind chest (presented by Sir Frederick Gore Ouseley).

Adding a proper Pedal Organ of 2½ octaves Compass CCC to F 30 notes with new Pedal board properly placed under Manuals - New Wind Chest for 3 stops with necessary action and movements using the former Pedal pipes as far as practicable containing:
1. Open Diapason 30 pipes 16ft. 2. Bourdon 30 pipes 16ft tone. 3. Spare for Trombone. Inserting 3 New Couplers Backfall movement in place of old Tumbler Couplers and an additional Coupler Swell to Pedals.

The Organ taken down and stowed away during progress of work in Church and afterwards removed to Factory in London to be remade - the whole of the pipes carefully revoiced, soldered up at tops and repaired where necessary. The Great Organ manuals recovered with new ivory. The action almost entirely new - new wind trunks and the whole of the interior work put in proper order. The instrument carefully regulated and tuned to equal temperament.

Making new frontage to organ of deal stained per Architect's design with upper part bracketted over, carved mouldings to as shewn and wrought iron standards and band enclosing front pipes.

The front pipes rearranged and altered to suit new design - necessary extra new pipes to complete frontage - new groove blocks and metal conveyances for ditto and alterations to present groove block etc. The front pipes and iron screen decorated in Gold and colours . . .

The additions and alterations carried out in the best manner and the instrument re-erected complete in the Church including the carriage but not enclosing any part of the back of organ.
£471.15.0

Extra work in decorating front pipes to Architect's design according to Architect's instructions. Gold edging to beyond what was contemplated in estimate.

£17.0.0.

John Horley transcribed the following work from Walker's order book for the period 1868 to 1891:

1868 June — Tuning and regulating the organ - 1870.

1870 April — The organ partly taken to pieces, pipes and soundboards taken out and rectifying damage done to the instrument by the rain having got inside. The whole regulated and tuned.

£13.15.0.

1872 Feb. — To rectifying considerable damage caused by wet. Taking the instrument partly to pieces the pipes taken out and the soundboard taken down and brought to factory re-worked and partly repalletted, the keyboard repaired and revoiced (sic). The movements sent to Factory and repaired. The pedalboard reworked. The whole carefully overhauled, regulated and tuned and put in good order.

£31.10.0.

1872 Aug. — Taking down organ and carefully stowing away same in Town Hall during rebuilding of Church.

£13.15.0.

Packing and erecting small organ in Town Hall for temporary use during rebuilding of Church.

£5.0.0.

1873 Dec. — Hire of said organ from Aug. 72 to this date, say 16 months at 30/- per month per agreement.

£24.0.0.

1874 June — To removing organ from Town Hall. The pipes and movements thoroughly cleaned, eased and the instrument carefully removed and re-erected in new position in Church. Arrangement of Front pipes altered to suit Arch of Pedal pipes at back to give head room. Bellows Handle altered to suit new position. The whole thoroughly overhauled and carefully regulated and tuned.

£54.10.0.

1874 — To taking down temporary organ, packing use of cases, etc. removing same to London, share of refixing etc.

£2.10.0.

1878 March — The organ partially cleaned from the dust and the temperament made to the "Equal system" and the whole of the instrument thoroughly overhauled, regulated and tuned.

£10.0.0.

1884 Aug. — The organ partly taken to pieces, pipes and movements eased and cleaned. The reed stops sent to factory, revoiced. The Pedal action quieted by inserting new felt, fresh buttons and cloths where necessary. The pipes reinstated and the whole thoroughly overhauled, regulated and put in good playing order.

£35.0.0.

The Organ tuned and regulated up to 1891

J. W. Walker was a popular choice of the Revd. Sir Frederick Gore Ouseley as an organ builder for his many schemes and for this and other reasons we can be sure that his advice was sought for the rebuilding of the organ in 1868. (*See* Chapter 5).

It would appear that in 1890 a report was submitted by J. W. Walker on the state of the organ which gave the sum of £500 as that which would be necessary to complete a major restoration of the instrument. As a result a fund was set up and by early 1894 £347.17s.0d. had been raised.

The contract for the work was, however, given to Frederick Rothwell, an organ builder whose address was in Hampstead at that time but who later moved to Harrow. Rothwell was well known for his ingenious organ consoles and other gadgets. His finest work was at St. George's Chapel, Windsor and the Temple Church, London. The work carried out at Dorking was quite modest and includes the replacement of the reed stops on the Great and Choir Organs. It was begun after the Choir Festival on 20 June 1894 and completed in time for a very late celebration of Harvest Festival on 11 November that year. By December 1894 the fund stood at £505.8s.5d. It is quite exceptional that as late as 1894 an organ of this size in a church of this status should remain hand blown.

In December 1894 Rothwell quoted an additional £75 for a pair of swell strings (Keraulophon and Voix Celeste) and a Vox Humana placed in its own box within the main Swell box. It took precisely ten years for this dream to be realised when once again the organ was cleaned. In October 1898 the Parish Magazine reported that the Organ Blowing Fund for a hydraulic system stood at £80.17s.0d. Although Mr Withers worked hard through the giving of many organ recitals (*see* Chapter 5) to raise the necessary funds to complete both the tonal scheme and the provision of a new blowing apparatus, it was the generosity of Lily, Duchess of Marlborough, which enabled this work to be completed in 1904.

At the PCC meeting held on 5 July, 1923, the Finance and General Purposes Committee reported that Mr Frederick Rothwell had met the committee and informed it that it was imperative that the organ be cleaned and recommended that instead of spending about £180 on just cleaning the organ the opportunity be taken, while the organ was dismantled, to bring it up to date by substituting tubular pneumatic action for the existing tracker work. He estimated the approximate cost at £950.

The Committee, at a subsequent meeting, thought they should have the opinion of other organ builders and Wm. Hill & Son, Norman and Beard Ltd., and J. W. Walker and Sons were asked for estimates and particulars of what should be done. Mr Rothwell was also asked for a definite price and specification.

The Committee reported that the following estimates had been received:
    Messrs Walker and Sons   £1,370 - £2,600 according to the scheme selected
    Hill, Norman and Beard   about £2,000
    Mr Frederick Rothwell   £1,027 - £1,165 according to the scheme selected

A decision was delayed for a further 12 months and in fact nothing further was done about the matter until 1928 when at the PCC meeting held on 5 December, Canon Newill, the vicar, stated that he had obtained tenders for the restoration of the organ as follows:
    Alfred Hunter   £2,350 - £2,750
    Hill, Norman and Beard   £2,040 - £2,700
    Frederick Rothwell   £1,648.

Both Hunter and Hill, Norman and Beard proposed to open the arch over the vestry into the north aisle. The Hunter scheme would have only incorporated seven stops from the present organ and increased the instrument to 39 speaking stops. Hill, Norman and Beard proposed that the console should be moved to the south side of the church. Rothwell was not prepared to consider any tonal changes or even to extend the manual compass. He even advised the continuation of a hydraulic blowing mechanism.

The following was Hill, Norman and Beard's report on the organ:-

"This Organ, although in fair useable condition now, is quite out of date in tonal design and mechanical control, and a thorough reconstruction is overdue. It is also suffering in every way from its cramped position so that a large amount of its present tone is lost by being smothered in a chamber with no outlet, except into an acoustically bad Chancel. No thought of rebuilding the present instrument or of installing a new instrument should be entertained that does not include the opening out of the west arch of chamber. This alteration would make it possible for the more powerful stops of Great, Swell and Pedal Organ to speak directly into the Church and produce space within the chamber for re-arrangement of pipes that are now almost useless from their cramped position.

The scheme we have submitted makes the best use of the present material at a very moderate outlay, and we have no doubt of a completely satisfactory result if our advice is accepted. The adoption of electric action will clear out of the chamber a mass of cumbersome action that now obstructs the tone.

The majority of the present material is sound, and after a thorough overhaul, entire tonal re-voicing and restoration, will give many years of effective service.

The alternative is an entirely new instrument at more than double the cost.

The disposal of the present instrument would be difficult, except at a considerable loss, owing to its size and construction.

Certain new additions to complete the scheme could be left out if funds are not sufficient, and could be inserted at a later date.

The present blowing plant will be quite inadequate for the rebuilt instrument, and we advise its replacement by electrically driven fans, and which we believe will cost much less to run than water, as two hydraulic engines would be required to supply the increased pressure.

In conclusion, we would beg to remind you that the cost of organs has increased by two and a half to three times the pre-war cost".

The scheme which Hill, Norman and Beard proposed in 1928 was similar to the work eventually executed in 1932/33. The proposals which were not carried out were for a new Claribel Flute stop on the Great Organ, a separate eight foot Horn stop on the Swell in addition to the present reed unit, a smaller and less interesting Choir Organ, a drawstop console and the major solo eight foot reed voiced on a pressure of twelve inches of wind. We have to be grateful that certain of these items never materialised five years later. The full scheme was published in the Parish Magazine of July 1929.

At the PCC meeting of 5 December 1928 already referred to, it was decided to ask Dr. Sydney Nicholson, the Warden of the School of English Church Music at Chislehurst,

Kent for his advice. He found in favour of Hill, Norman and Beard and dismissed Frederick Rothwell's proposals without any further comment. Dr. Edward C. Bairstow, the organist of York Minster, endorsed Dr. Nicholson's comments and so the parish began the work of collecting the required sum of £2,500.

Dr. Nicholson's notes written on the side of Hill, Norman and Beard's estimate and returned to Canon Newill on 12 December 1928 display his personal preferences for 'as much plain pneumatic (action) as possible or arrangements should be made that, if the electric current for the action failed some of the organ should at least be available' and 'a detached console should be avoided if possible'.

The damage resulting from the great storm of December 1929 when the top of the spire collapsed, the sudden need for the provision of a new Duplex blower, fitted during January 1931, and inflation resulting from the collapse of the stock market in 1929/30 held up the collection of the required sum, so that it became necessary in May 1932 to consult with Hill, Norman and Beard to produce a revised estimate and proceed on the basis of the £2,000 in hand. Trollope and Colls Ltd estimated on 25 May 1932 the sum of £8.5s.0d. for the removal of the required masonry and making good the arch over the vestry in preparation for the new organ case. The Diocese recommended a plainer design for that case-work and finally granted the faculty on 23 July 1932.

The work began on Monday 15 August 1932 and the refurbished instrument was dedicated by the Bishop of Guildford during the service of confirmation on 30 March 1933. The organ builder's bill was for £2,030. The final £30 was the cost of the duplication of the Great Trumpet on the Choir manual.

One of the problems which was created by the 1933 rebuilding of the organ was the position of the console. This was placed in the north-west corner of the Lady Chapel facing east, a position that was undoubtedly excellent for the ability to direct the choir but difficult for assessing the balance between organ and choir. With the screen then between the nave and chancel, it was also difficult to see a conductor in a choral society performance. The best position for solving these problems would have been to place the console in front of the font at the west end!

At the meeting of the PCC on 8 December 1950 Dr. William Cole gave the particulars of an estimate for £579 from Hill, Norman and Beard as the cost for cleaning the instrument and lowering the pitch. It was passed by the meeting and decided that the work should be put in hand in August 1951. By September 1951 the cost had risen to £653. Although there is no evidence available in writing, it has always been assumed that Dr. Ralph Vaughan Williams urged Dr. Cole to suggest the removal of the console to its present position in the south aisle. The proposal was passed by the PCC on 21 September 1951 on a temporary basis. The completion of the work on the organ was marked by a recital given on 4 November 1951 by Dr. William McKie, organist of Westminster Abbey.

Further work proved necessary in 1970 when a considerable amount was spent on the leatherwork and the re-ordering of the Second Principal Stop (4ft) on the Great Organ as a Twelfth ($2\frac{2}{3}$) stop.

From 1984 onwards the instrument began to display a degree of unreliability. In the spring of 1986 the Combined Church Council took the decision to spend £51,000 on the organ. The electro pneumatic action had begun to fail and the fear of imminent breakdown initiated swift action. Three organ builders were consulted, Rushworth and Dreaper of Liverpool, Kenneth James and Hill, Norman and Beard. Once again Hill, Norman and Beard Ltd were given the contract to undertake the work of replacing the action with a solid state system and making certain tonal adjustments. The work began on Monday, 4 August, 1986 and was substantially completed for the services on Sunday 14 December 1986. While the instrument was being rebuilt, a two rank chamber organ on loan from Hill, Norman and Beard was in use.

The console was remodelled with a new dual track system of pistons including six general pistons to all stops and couplers, all adjustable by the 'setter' button under the Choir key bench. The pipework was cleaned and restored throughout. The opportunity was taken to make certain tonal changes to overcome the alterations made to the acoustical properties of the chancel in the 1960s when the screen was removed and a carpet laid. To this end attention was given to the upperwork by re-ordering the Great and Swell Mixture stops, rescaling the Swell Fifteenth stop and, by a simple process of rewiring, altering the top of the Choir Dulciana unit from a Tierce ($1\frac{3}{5}$ft) to a Twenty Second (1ft). To aid the clarity of the Pedal line a 4 ft Choral Bass stop took the place of the trebles of the overscaled Great Large Open Diapason in the north aisle case. The Swell and Great reed stops were revoiced. The Posaune (8ft) has been voiced as a small scale Tuba and suited more to that solo role rather than a chorus reed. Preparation has been made on the Great soundboard for the addition of a small scale chorus reed and a 4ft Flute stop. The action is also present in the system and a blank stop key included in the stop jamb. The Posaune remains temporarily joined to the Great Organ department. The Acoustic 32ft stop on the Pedal Organ was removed.

The organ was rededicated on Saturday 21 February 1987 by the Archdeacon of Dorking and a recital was given that evening by Dr. Francis Jackson O.B.E., formerly Organist and Master of the Choristers at York Minster.

The Specification of the Organ from December 1986

(The specifications of the organ in 1868, 1894 and 1933 may be found in the Dorking and District Museum).

Great Organ
CC-C 61 notes

1894/1933	1.	Contra Geigen		m	16ft
1831	2.	Open Diapason I		m	8ft
1831	3.	Open Diapason II		m	8ft
1831	4.	Stopped Diapason		w	8ft
1831	5.	Octave		m	4ft
—	6.	Flute	prepared for	—	4ft
1831/1970	7.	Octave Quint		m	$2\frac{2}{3}$ft
1831	8.	Super Octave		m	2ft
1986	9.	Mixture	22, 26, 29	—	
1894	10.	Posaune	Choir	—	8ft
			Swell to Great		
			Choir to Great		

Swell Organ
CC-C 61 notes

1868	1.	Bourdon		w	16ft
1831/1868	2.	Open Diapasaon		w/m	8ft
1904	3.	Salicional		m	8ft
1904	4.	Vox Angelica	Tenor C	m	8ft
1831	5.	Stopped Diapason		w	8ft
1831	6.	Principal		m	4ft
1894	7.	Harmonic Flute		m	4ft (ex Great Organ)
1933	8.	Fifteenth		m	2ft
1986	9.	Mixture	22, 26	—	
1868	10.	Oboe		m	8ft
			Tremulant		
1933	11.	Contra Fagotto	85 pipes	m	16ft
1933	12.	Trumpet	No 11	—	8ft
1933	13.	Clarion	No 11	—	4ft

Octave
Sub Octave
Unison Off

Choir Organ (enclosed)
CC-C 61 notes

1933	1.	Contra Dulciana (Tenor C) 85 pipes		m	16ft
1933	2.	Viol d'Orchestre		m	8ft
1894	3.	Wald Flute (Bottom octave stopped)		w	8ft
1831/1894	4.	Dulciana	No 1	—	8ft
1831	5.	Stopped Flute		w	4ft
1933	6.	Dulcet	No 1	—	4ft
1933	7.	Nazard (Tenor C)		m	$2\frac{2}{3}$ft
1868	8.	Flautina		w	2ft
1933	9.	Dulcetina	No 1	—	2ft
1986	10.	Twenty Second	No 1	—	1ft
1894	11.	Clarinet		m	8ft
			Tremulant		

(unenclosed)

1894	12.	Posaune		m	8ft

Octave
Sub Octave
Unison Off
Swell to Choir

Pedal Organ
CCC-G 32 notes

1831/1868	1.	Open Wood Bass	42 pipes	w	16ft
1933	2.	Geigen Bass	Great	—	16ft

1868	3.	Sub Bass	42 pipes	w	16ft
1933	4.	Bourdon	Swell	—	16ft
1933	5.	Octave Wood	No 1	—	8ft
1894	6.	Geigen Principal	Great No 1	—	8ft
1933	7.	Bass Flute	No 3	—	8ft
1986	8.	Choral Bass	32 pipes	m	4ft
1894	9.	Trombone	32 pipes	m	16ft
1933	10.	Contra Fagotto	Swell	—	16ft

Swell to Pedal
Great to Pedal
Choir to Pedal
Great and Pedal Combinations Coupled

Accessories
5 thumb pistons to each manual division
5 toe pistons to pedal
5 toe pistons duplicating the Swell thumb pistons
6 general pistons to all stops and couplers
All pistons are adjustable at the console by setter piston (dual track system)
Reversible thumb pistons:
Swell to Great; Swell to Choir; Swell to Pedal; Great to Pedal; Choir to Pedal
Reversible toe piston and bar:
Great to Pedal
General cancel piston

The Bells

Very little is known of the early history of the bells, but in 1552 Edward VI appointed the Marquis of Northampton and several other gentlemen to examine the state of 'church goodes' and to ascertain and preserve the property found in churches and to prevent it being 'embesiled and removed'. In Dorking parish church the list included:-

"Item v belles in the steple, the best by estimacion xvi c and the resydew under
   after the rate
Item a chyme
Item iiij handbelles
All of which is commytted to the custody of Robert Auncell William Goodwyn John
   Hether and John Hoker the sixte of October in the sixte yere of the raine of our
   said soveraigne Lorde."

None of these bells exists today, the oldest in the tower being No. 5 which is dated 1626 and was made by John Wilner of Ightham, Kent. Five others of the present ring of eight must have rung in the medieval church - Nos. 2, 3 (re-cast in 1955) and 4, all made by Richard Phelps in 1709; No. 8 by Robert Catlin in 1746 and No. 7 by Thomas Mears in 1827. The remaining two bells, Nos. 1 and 6, were made by Thomas Mears in 1837 and 1842, early in the life of the Intermediate Church, but these must have been replacements because J. S. Bright in his book, *A History of Dorking*, 1884, quotes from a letter of about 1710 from the Revd. S. Highmore, Minister of the Non-Conformist Church, Dorking, and then in the British Museum:

"We have a good ring of eight bells, and value ourselves very much upon it".

This suggests that the installation of the three new bells in 1709 was quite an event in the town which, some 60 years later, had a population of only 1800.

A writer in the Gentleman's Magazine for May 1763 stated that "The church is a plain stone building, and has a tower steeple in which there is a ring of eight small but tunable bells, with a set of chimes". As the tenor bell, which had been installed in 1746, weighs over a ton, it is difficult to believe they were small bells!

Vestry Minutes are a great source of information. At a Vestry "holden for the Parish aforesaid the first of June and in the Year of our Lord 1742" we read:

" . . . it is agreed their (sic) shall be but Six days for Ringing to be payd for by the Churchwardens as follows - Restoration; The Coronation and Birthday of the King; the fifth of November and Christmas Day and the Prince's Birthday."

and at the next Vestry held on 6 June 1742 this was repeated, with the addition of:

"That the Charges for looking after the clocke Chimes be four Pounds a Year and for digging the Graves & Ringing the Bell for Parish Burials at two Shillings each. That for ringing the sixth Bell for the Burying any poor person of this Parish be allowed this same price."

The inscriptions on our bells provide a list of prominent Dorking people. There are three vicars: Philip Walton, George Feachem and James Joyce. The three bells given in 1709 bear the donors' names. Two were given by Mrs Margaret Fenwicke and her husband William of Betchworth Castle and the other by John Hollier and John Finney. Churchwardens mentioned include Edward Ansell, Richard Rose, James Dewdney, John Bartlett, John Marshall and James White, all well known professional men and tradesmen in the town.

The weight of St. Martin's bells varies between $4\frac{3}{4}$cwt (240Kgs) and 23cwt (1.2 metric tonnes), a total of over 4 tons. They have a lovely tone, but it does mean that young people cannot be taught until they have the necessary height and strength. Today's bells are mounted on ballbearings which have taken much of the hard work out of ringing, a good thing in these days of equal numbers of men and women ringers. During the First World War when the male ringers were "called up" the verger, Mr Edward Dodd, who was also Captain of Bells, was the first to train an all-ladies band.

Frequently in the past there were differences of opinion between the church authorities and the ringers, many of whom used the bells for their own pleasure and amusement. In 1889 new Rules for the St. Martin's Guild of Bellringers were drawn up and signed by the vicar and churchwardens, who are responsible for the bells and the belfry. These emphasised that all ringers were expected to attend the services of the church and to lead "Godly and Christian lives as being Officers of the Church in which they ring". A fine of 1 shilling was made on any ringer being a $\frac{1}{4}$ hour late for service and 3d. for being late for practice, all fines having to be paid within a fortnight. A fine of 6d. was imposed for improper and abusive language or conduct. No dogs were allowed in the belfry. Even these rules did not prevent the vicar losing patience with his bellringers in 1897, as is recorded in the section on 'Canon Chichester'. (*See* Chapter 4).

A full peal of 5040 changes takes over 3 hours to ring. The earliest peal board in the belfry is dated 1838 and would therefore have been the first rung in the recently rebuilt Intermediate Church. Any older boards must have been demolished with the old church. It reads:

December 31st 1838

was rung in this Steeple a True & Complete Peal of 5040 Changes of Grandsire Trebles in Three Hours Four Minutes by Four Senr & Four Junr Youths of this Parish. It being the first anniversary of New Year's Eve since the erection of the new Church.

		Age
Treble	Chas. Boxall	17
2	Jno Fuller	41
3	Jno Gurnett	34
4	Hy Bravery	64
5	Willm Dale	41
6	Jos Fuller	35
7	Geo Gurnett	72
Tenor	Benj Rose	19

Conducted by Mr Jno Fuller

Again, a lot of old Dorking names. From the list of ages it would seem that a 'Junior Youth' became a 'Senior Youth' around the age of 40!

Other peals were rung for Queen Victoria's wedding day in 1840; the first in the present tower in 1878; on the occasion of the laying of the foundation stone of the extended Lady Chapel in December 1912 and another for its dedication in March 1913. A peal was rung for the signing of Peace on 8 July 1919 and another for the signing of the Armistice Terms on 11 November 1922. Others were rung over the years just for the pleasure of the ringers.

In the 18th and 19th centuries special ringing took place at Dorking on Shrove Tuesday, when a 'Pancake' bell was rung between 11 a.m. and 12 noon prior to the Shrove Tuesday Football match, and in the early years of the 20th century a Death Bell was still being rung.

When the present church was built, the bells were taken down from the central tower. They were finally re-hung in the new west tower in 1877, wholly at the expense of Mrs. Burt of Pippbrook House, who also charged herself with the presentation of an entirely new clock, the old one being found very difficult to fit in with the new arrangement of the bells. This clock was driven by heavy weights which dropped from the clock chamber to the west door. The verger had to climb up several times a week and manually wind them up, a very laborious task. Eventually, in 1962, it was decided to convert the clock to electric drive. Each time a mechanic comes to service the clock he seems to have a different idea of the sequence of the chimes, but the original arrangement is

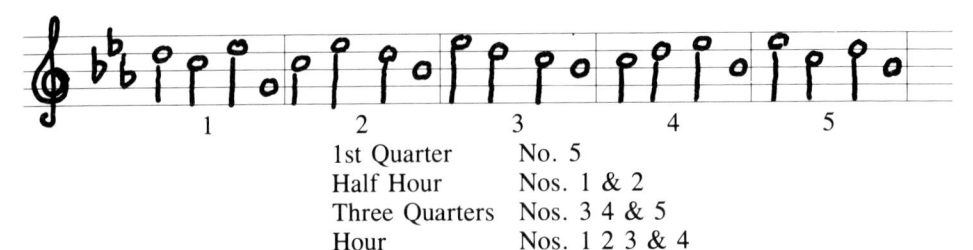

1st Quarter	No. 5
Half Hour	Nos. 1 & 2
Three Quarters	Nos. 3 4 & 5
Hour	Nos. 1 2 3 & 4

Outside, the clock has three dials facing north, west and south, and between them are the words carved in stone "OMNIA HABENT TEMPORA, PEREUNT ET IMPUTANTUR". They are generally interpreted as "All things have their season, go by and are placed to their account". In the corners surrounding the dials on the west face is carved 1873, the date when the foundation stone of the tower was laid.

So, how better to sum up our bells and clock and our pride in them than to remember the Revd. S. Highmore's words written nearly 300 years ago.

Chapter 4

Some Priests and People

The Reverend James Joyce

The year 1837, when the Revd. James Joyce received the living of Dorking from the Duke of Norfolk, also saw the new young Queen ascend the throne. He was therefore the first vicar of Dorking in the Victorian era and, according to a memoir left by his eldest son, was well suited to the times. He was born in 1781, and was an Oxford graduate and an extremely erudite man. He had, in addition to a knowledge of Hebrew, Greek and Latin, familiarity with several European languages. More unusually, perhaps, he possessed a great aptitude for, and interest in, mathematics. His great-grandson, Sir Stephen Tallents, also refers to him as a 'scholarly clergyman of Irish descent, who combined his parish work as vicar with coaching private pupils for the University.' As noted in Chapter 5, one of his pupils was the musical prodigy, Frederick Gore Ouseley.

James Joyce took up his duties at a time of social, political and religious change in the country at large, but he also found important local changes, as one of his first duties was to arrange the consecration of the 'Intermediate Church', which had been built during 1835-1837, to replace the nave and aisles of the medieval structure. He was active in church matters and was said by Neville Stiff to have 'raised the tone of things' in the town and district. One of his first actions was to hold a vestry meeting 'to determine once and for all the different duties of the parish clerk, sexton and beadle'. This resulted in the replacement of the 'slovenly clerk' and unsatisfactory sexton!

From 1839 James Joyce occupied the vicarage at the junction of Vincent Lane and Westcott Road, when this was secured from W. J. Denison. The previous vicar, Mr. Feachem, had lived in a house in South Street, which has sadly been demolished. The new vicarage, a handsome house still standing, but no longer the vicarage, at that time stood in a semi rural setting as Vincent Lane was then, in the words of Charles Rose, a 'pretty shady retreat resounding with the song of birds and with banks bespangled with flowers'. The vicar can be imagined making his way along the picturesque streets of the old town to reach St. Martin's church.

His time as vicar coincided with a general resurgence of interest in the life of the church. One of the first results of this was the subdivision of large old parishes, and the building of new parish churches. During the period that James Joyce was vicar the parishes of Holmwood and Coldharbour were formed out of the parish of St. Martin's. In both cases the churches were built through the generosity of prominent local residents, Holmwood church being consecrated in 1838 and Coldharbour in 1848.

James Joyce was still vicar of Dorking when he died suddenly in October 1850, having preached a sermon only a few days previously. He was buried in St. Martin's churchyard, near the west boundary, where a handsome gravestone can still be seen and there is a memorial tablet to him now placed in the tower. A memorial window in the Lady Chapel to him and his wife testifies to the strong links between him and the Cubitts of Denbies. His youngest daughter Laura, who married Mr. George Cubitt and later became the first Lady Ashcombe, presented this fine window in 1874.

The Reverend William Henry Joyce

The Revd. William Henry Joyce was born in 1817 and educated at Charterhouse and Oxford. He was ordained in 1842, and assisted his father as curate from that year until 1848. He then succeeded to the living on the sudden death of his father in 1850. Thus for a period of 33 years St. Martin's church was served by members of the same family. The connections with the Joyce family were indeed stronger than that, as William Joyce's elder brother, the Revd. John Wayland Joyce, had been curate to his father from 1838 to 1843, and later his nephew, the Revd. James Barclay Joyce, son of John Wayland, also served as a curate at St. Martin's from 1875 to 1876, while the Revd. Peter Righton Atkinson was vicar.

Mr. Joyce was a popular figure in the town, being in Stiff's words of 'singular charm and gentleness of manner'. He had been at Oxford during the start of the Tractarian movement, which must have influenced him greatly. He was a keen student of theology, a man of strong opinions and a High Churchman. He was responsible for the institution of a Sunday evening service and of the three-hour Good Friday service. He also ensured that the church was kept open day by day for private prayer and the daily offices. He married in 1859 and his wife was also a well known and popular figure in the town, and an excellent nurse who would take care of the sick poor in those days of sketchy medical services.

On a practical level, Mr. Joyce also endeavoured to ensure that the church and churchyard were maintained in a good condition, which in earlier years of the century had not always been the case. Stiff reported that at one time 'the churchyard . . . owing to the numberless doors and gates opening on to it had been used as a "drying ground" for the clothes of the surrounding dwellers, also as a rubbish heap, &c.' This theme is repeated in the Parish Magazine as late as 1875, when it was reported that good iron railings had been erected at the south-eastern corner of the churchyard, and shrubs and trees planted, thus rescuing it from squalor and neglect.

The most important decision taken during his time as vicar, however, was to replace the medieval chancel of St. Martin's church with the present one, which was donated by W. H. Forman (*see* Chapter 3). We are told that on the day of consecration, 30 April 1868, Mr. Joyce had the seven sanctuary lamps lighted, and they were never allowed to go out in his time.

The formation of new parishes out of that of St. Martin's and the building of new churches to serve them also continued. During W. H. Joyce's time as vicar the parish of St. Paul's, Dorking, was formed in the southern part of the town, the church being consecrated in 1857. The parish of Westcott had also been formed in 1852 and that of Ranmore, partly out of St. Martin's, in 1860. The church at Ranmore was built in 1859 by Mr. George Cubitt, later the first Lord Ashcombe, and Mr. Joyce's brother-in-law, as the estate church to his mansion of Denbies.

William Joyce died at the relatively early age of 53, leaving his widow with six young children. He was much mourned in the town and, as with his father, there is a memorial tablet to him, now placed in the tower. Also a memorial window in the south aisle, plus others in the clerestory, were placed in St. Martin's in 1875 by parishioners and friends.

William Henry Forman and Elizabeth Forman

In 1849 the fine old estate of Pippbrook, on the town's eastern boundaries, was put up for sale: the consequences, for the development of the church of St. Martin and for the parish, proved to be important and incalculable.

A century earlier, in the 1750s, William Page had built at Pippbrook a classical house of three storeys; a painting, now hanging in a committee room at Lords Cricket Ground, shows this house standing in extensive gardens, with the hills to the south in the distance. However, few of the succeeding occupiers stayed for more than a few years until the property passed into the ownership of William Crawford, M.P. for the City of London and chairman of the Dorking bench. On his death Pippbrook passed to his son, R. W. Crawford, who succeeded his father as M.P. for the City, and when he put the estate up for sale in 1849 it was purchased by Thomas Seaton Forman.

This gentleman had been M.P. for Bridgwater in Somerset, from 1841 until his retirement in 1847, his addresses at that time being given as Albany Court Yard, London, and Pen-y-daran Place, Glamorganshire. There is no indication of why he chose to reside in Dorking, but at that date many wealthy people were choosing to buy or build in the leafy Home Counties, which had become easily accessible to the capital via the recently opened railways.

Thomas Seaton Forman was then aged 58, the eldest son of William Forman, who died in 1829, and Mary, his wife, deceased in 1804. William was a wine merchant in Doncaster when he married Mary Seaton who was a member of a leading local family. He was also an ordnance agent at the Tower of London when he became a partner in the Penydarren Iron Company, which was founded by Francis Homfray and his sons in 1784, the last of the four great Merthyr ironworks to open.

William Forman moved to Penydarren House in 1813 when he took charge of the works. Two other brothers were associated with him there, and clearly they made a great deal of money. However, family members continued to be buried in the Seaton vault, beneath the south chapel of the ancient church of St. George, in Doncaster, and an inscription in the south-west window of the present chapel reads: 'To the memory of Thomas Seaton Forman Esq. of Pippbrook House, Dorking, Surrey . . . . who died at Pisa in Italy on 30 December 1850, aged 59, and was buried in this chapel 10 March 1851'.

Thomas had enjoyed his Dorking retreat for barely a year: it was to be his brother, William Henry Forman, then aged 57, who was to play such a significant role in the future. Pippbrook was willed to him by his elder brother, although Thomas's widow, Elizabeth, was to continue to reside in the house. Indeed, the census returns of 1851 and 1861 both name her as 'Head of House', while William Forman is shown as 'Visitor', 'Unmarried' and 'Proprietor of Iron Mines' on both occasions.

Elizabeth, described simply as 'Annuitant', was thirty-eight years old in 1851. There is no record of any children of the marriage. Living with her was her sister, Hannah Moore, six years younger, but there is a discrepancy regarding her status, in the census returns: in 1851 she is shown as 'married', in 1861 as 'unmarried'. Both sisters were born in Shrewsbury.

The unassuming 'visitor', and sole owner of Pippbrook, William Henry Forman, had become an Iron Master like his father, and was very rich, with an estimated establishment at that time of between four and five million pounds. In 1853 he read a newspaper account of the destruction by fire on 28 February of the church of St. George, in Doncaster, his birthplace. He immediately wrote to the Diocesan authorities and offered to re-build the south chapel, at his own expense, which was thenceforward known as the Forman chapel. The architect chosen to re-build the ruined church was George Gilbert Scott, whose preliminary designs were completed by the end of 1853, so when William decided to transform his Dorking property into a treasure-house, fit to receive and display the exquisite and valuable objects he had collected in his travels all over the world, it was once again to the renowned architect that he turned. George Gilbert Scott's preliminary design and contract drawings for the new Pippbrook House are dated 1855. Scott's design was for a gaunt but undoubtedly striking gothic revival mansion, with mullioned and transomed windows, decorated cornices, and a richly carved and painted interior.

Perhaps it was the contemplation of his two triumphant building enterprises, in Doncaster and in Dorking, that led William Forman to make a generous offer, so much to the benefit of the church and people. It followed the death of Hannah Moore, Elizabeth Forman's sister, in April 1866. She was buried in the Forman chapel in St. George's, Doncaster, and after the service, for which the vicar of Dorking had travelled north, in order to officiate, Elizabeth told the Revd. W. H. Joyce that her brother-in-law had proposed the re-building of the chancel of St. Martin's Church, for which he would bear the cost. This was quickly put in hand, and the east window records the building and decoration of the chancel in memory of Anne (sic) Moore by William Henry Forman and is dated 1867. (*See* Chapter 3. This window depicts scenes from the Passion and Resurrection and contains two small shields with arms of the Forman and Seaton families.

During the re-building, on the 27 June 1867, Elizabeth was married, by special licence, to Major Thomas Seymour Burt, and thenceforward it is the name of Elizabeth Burt which recurs in church and parish annals. Her husband, Thomas Seymour Burt, was born in 1805, younger son of the Revd. Charles Henry Burt, vicar of Cannington, near Bridgwater in Somerset. He was commissioned lieutenant in the Bengal Engineers in 1824. In 1825 he went to India, where he spent much of his Army career, being promoted to Captain in 1834 and Major in 1843; he is listed as 'Suptng. Eng.' in Sind, in 1844. But in June 1847 he was tried by a General Court Martial, at Allahabad, for an unspecified offence, and was dismissed the service. Such an abrupt end to an apparently successful career is even more inexplicable when one learns that a decade earlier he had been made a Fellow of the Royal Society: his certificate of entry, in March 1836, describes him as . . . . 'of the Bengal Engineers, of Manchester St., Manchester Square, author of various scientific reports on scientific subjects in the Journal of the Asiatic Society of Bengal'. Following his return from India he publised *A satirical epitome of the history of England, prior to the reign of George I*, in 1852, and three volumes of 'Miscellaneous papers on scientific subjects, written chiefly in India'.

His marriage and move to Dorking seems to have inspired further writing: in November he contributed a poem 'To Sabine, Pippbrook House, Dorking', to the Journal of the Royal Society, and two years later a paper on 'a discovery I have lately made in the power and

Bishop Wilberforce (1805-1873) who laid the foundation stone of the west tower in 1873, an oil painting by G. Richmond c1864.

The clergy at St. Martin's, seen in the garden of the Vicarage, seated left to right, the Vicar, Archdeacon P. R. Atkinson, and curates the Revds. G. Hughes and H. W. Brock, standing left to right, curates the Revds. L. H. Burrows, L. R. Flood and R. C. Lott, a photograph taken c1881.

effect of the lens or magnifying glass'. Finally, in 1883, came two works which must have preoccupied him during the previous decade; one volume is listed in the Royal Society Library Catalogue as *The Aeneid, Georgics and Eclogues of Virgil rendered into English blank verse;* the other is entitled *The Christian's Pattern, or a Treatise on the Imitation of Christ written in Latin by Thomas à Kempis, abridged and published by the Reverend John Wesley and now rendered into Blank Verse* by T. S. Burt, F.R.S./M.R.A.S. A leather-bound copy of this laborious work may be seen in Dorking Museum Library, the fly-leaf bearing the inscription, 'the following work is Most Affectionately Dedicated to my wife, Elizabeth Burt, who has taken so Great an Interest in its Contents and their Production'. The author's Preface notes that 'previously to my leaving Allahabad in the Upper Provinces of India . . . . my kind friend, the late Major-General Archibald Watson, Commandant of the Garrison, asked me to accept . . . . the copy of a pocket edition of the Imitation of Christ . . . . It was only in 1873 that I had it in my power thoroughly to go through its pages . . . . I had in the interim seen a larger and fuller copy of the Imitation which the Vicar of Dorking, Reverend Joyce, had kindly presented to my wife on the occasion of our marriage by special license . . . .'

In all the foregoing there is no direct clue to the mystery of Major Burt's dismissal from service, in the prime of his life. But the census returns of 1871, and 1881 place an asterisk beside his name, with the laconic note below: 'lunatic'. Here, then, is the substance of the shadow across his life. The 1871 census shows George Dodsworth, a member of the Royal College of Surgeons, as a 'boarder' at Pippbrook and he must be assumed to be the Major's personal physician. In 1881 William Holman is listed as 'Attendant' (his brother, Frank, is a footman) and the Major's obituary notice, in the *Surrey Advertiser,* records that he 'had been ill for some years and attended by Dr. Charles Chaldecott'. Certainly this explains why local newspapers and magazines, although they continue to refer to Mrs Burt, make no mention of her husband.

In 1869, two years after Elizabeth's marriage, William Forman died at Fonthill House, in Tunbridge Wells. He left Pippbrook House to his sister-in-law, in succession to other members of his family, and she is shown as 'Head of House' in 1871, although her husband is, finally, so designated in the 1881 census. Elizabeth continued to give generously to St. Martin's and its people. She helped particularly with the final efforts to complete the rebuilding of the church, contributing £300 towards the spire. Then in 1877 she bore the whole cost of re-hanging the bells, which had been silent since 1872, and the following year she presented a new clock since the old one was difficult to work with the new arrangement of the bells.

Elizabeth's death, on 5 July 1889, at the age of seventy-five, is recorded in the inscription on the Burt Memorial in St. George's Church, Doncaster, in the Forman Chapel where she was interred. Her husband survived her for less than a year; sadly, it seems there was a family dispute over the Pippbrook inheritance and Major Burt died at Cotmandene, although he was buried with his wife. The estate was sold by auction, in four lots, in 1891 by order of the Court of Chancery. So ended the fruitful association of the Formans and the Burts with St. Martin's Church.

Canon Chichester

Edward Arthur Chichester was born on 23 February 1849, the eldest son of the Revd. George Vaughan Chichester, Rector of Wotton. They were descended from Sir Arthur Chichester, Lord Deputy of Ireland in the reign of James I. In the early nineteenth century several members of the family were clergymen, and in 1855, his uncle, the Revd. William Chichester, inherited the estates of the O'Neill family and was created first Baron O'Neill.

The Revd. Neville Stiff was curate to Mr. Chichester between 1911 and 1913 and has therefore dealt quite fully in his book with the early years of Mr. Chichester's vicariate of St. Martin's Church, so any repetition here will be brief.

He was educated at St. John's College, Cambridge, and received his B.A. degree in 1872, to be followed by M.A. in 1883. In 1875 he was ordained deacon in St. Martin's Church and went to Farncombe for two years. He was ordained priest in 1876 by Dr. Harold Browne, Bishop of Winchester, and the following year was appointed vicar of Okewood where he remained until 1885 when he came to Dorking. In the previous year he had married Mary Agnes Cubitt, daughter of the Rt. Hon. George Cubitt, M.P., later the first Lord Ashcombe. The ceremony was conducted by the Archbishop of Canterbury, Dr. Benson, who had been an old College friend of the bride's father. They had two daughters and two sons, one of whom was killed in action in 1916, the other, Arthur O'Neill Cubitt Chichester, a Lieutenant-Colonel of the Surrey Yeomanry, married and settled in Northern Ireland on his wife's estate.

From 1891 to 1919 Mr. Chichester was Rural Dean and in 1906 he was made an Honorary Canon of Winchester Cathedral, an office vacated by Canon Utterton, Vicar of Leatherhead, on being appointed Archdeacon of Surrey. Despite his request that his friends should address him as formerly, he became "Canon Chichester" to all Dorking thereafter.

When the young Edward Chichester came to Dorking in 1885 it was to a very lively and active parish. There were two experienced curates, the Revd. R. C. Lott and the Revd. Leonard H. Burrows, who became Bishop of Lewes and, later, of Sheffield. There was an excellent choir under Mr. Withers, a large Sunday school and many societies and clubs involving all sections of the congregation. This is evidenced by the fact that within months of his arrival 106 of the 265 candidates for confirmation were members of St. Martin's Church, and the number of Easter communicants was 774. Nevertheless there was still much to be done, both within the church and outside in the town.

One of the first things he did was to make all seats in church free after the 5 minute bell had begun, and the little brass plates which are still on some of the pew ends were put there to show that the previous "tenants" had given up their exclusive right to sit in those seats. It probably followed that the church filled up a good five minutes before the service!

A Mission held in January 1890 led to a growing list of social, religious and educational activities in the church. Dinners for invalids were served every Friday, a cup of coffee or cocoa and two slices of bread and butter or cake were available in the Coffee Room for 2d, and a Parish Nursing Association supplied nurses. He was active in furthering the decoration of the recently rebuilt church. In 1889 a stained glass window was placed in the south aisle as a memorial to Archdeacon Atkinson. 1892 saw the erection of the central part of the mosaic over the chancel arch; several memorial windows were added, followed by the marble tablets recording Vicars, Bishops and Archbishops, and the mosaic marking Queen Victoria's Jubilee (*see* the Present Church and Furnishings).

Canon Chichester was a fluent and vigorous preacher and had the courage to voice his convictions. In 1889 he introduced a series of "mid-day talks to busy men" which proved very popular. All the interests of the town were his, especially matters concerning education. He supported denominational education in the elementary schools. He was the first Chairman of the Dorking High School for Boys and it was largely due to his strenuous efforts and enthusiasm that it grew and flourished. Some years later the need for a Girls' High School was felt and as Chairman of the Management Committee he steered this through all the difficulties of accommodation and recognition by the Board of Education. The Dorking Hospital was close to his heart. With finances at a low ebb his cheerful optimism helped to raise the efficiency of the Hospital, the equipment was improved to cope with the advancement of medical and surgical science, and finally there was a fund raising appeal for an enlargement scheme.

Other interests were the Dorking Charities, of which he was Chairman; he was keenly concerned with the well-being of the inmates of the Almshouses and the poor in the Infirmary. He took a great interest in the N.S.P.C.C. He was one of the oldest Past Masters of the Dorking Freemasonry Lodge. With all this he found time to relax with a fishing rod and spent many enjoyable hours in wielding the fly on the waters of Mount pond on the Denbies estate, which at one time was noted for its fine trout. In later years he enjoyed a game of bowls and was a Vice President of the Dorking Club.

In 1905/6 a new chapel was carved out of the south transept. Canon Chichester reached 25 years of his ministry at St. Martin's in 1910, and when the question of a suitable gift was considered, he was delighted to accept the suggestion of extending the Chapel eastwards. The stained glass windows between the chancel and chapel are a reminder that this was originally an outside wall. The consecration took place in March 1913 but the formal presentation was in November of that year at a social gathering in the Drill Hall of nearly 900 parishioners and others associated with St. Martin's. Mr. W. J. Down in his presentation speech said that while they had not seen eye to eye on many occasions, there was no better man to differ from than their vicar. Canon Chichester in his reply stressed that without the support and backing of the churchwardens and helpers and workers in every part of the parish he could have achieved very little. While he was speaking there was a commotion caused by Mr. J. W. Moorhouse taking a flashlight photograph, and he assured the people that it was not the work of suffragettes! He was also presented with a book containing the signatures of all the subscribers to the chapel.

When he came to Dorking Canon Chichester was very much an Anglican and had little time for the independent or non-conformist Churches. The Revd. T. Grantham of the Congregational Church recalled how some three years after he had come to Dorking he still had not met or spoken to the Canon until one Sunday when they were the only two passengers on a train to Dorking. He was returning from a preaching appointment in Southampton and the Canon from taking a service in Winchester Cathedral. Before he could make the first advance Canon Chichester met him with a smile and handshake saying "I think we are from the same town". Mr. Grantham replied "Yes, and we ought to have greeted each other before". From that day they drew closer to each other, but Mr.

Grantham knew that the Canon considered there was no need for an Independent church in the town.

The Canon's genial and kindly nature was the velvet glove over an iron hand and he did not hestitate to speak or act in support of his convictions. In 1897 he locked the bellringers out of the belfry because of the habitually late arrival of some of the ringers "which militated against the punctual attendance of the congregation". There was no ringing for Queen Victoria's Diamond Jubilee nor for New Year's Eve which caused quite a stir in the town. The *Daily Mail* heard of this and wrote to the Vicar asking for his version of the affair. The reply came — "Jan 10 1897. Dear Sir, In reply to yours of 9th, there is no band of bellringers at Dorking. Yours truly".

Canon Chichester retired in 1921, partly because of ill health, and lived at Ashleigh, Westhumble, until his death on 1 October 1925. In the long history of St. Martin's church there is no record of a parish priest serving the church as devotedly for so many years, and as beloved by his parishioners and the townsfolk as Canon Edward Chichester.

Lily, Duchess of Marlborough

Lily, Duchess of Marlborough, daughter of Commodore Price of the US Navy, came to the Deepdene, Dorking, in 1894 and made it her home until her death in 1909. Although only 54 when she died, she had outlived three husbands. The first, American businessman Louis Hammersley, brought her great wealth; the second, the 8th Duke of Marlborough, bestowed on her a title (which she continued to use as a courtesy for the rest of her life); the third, Lord William Beresford, VC, gave her greatest happiness and, in 1897, the son she had longed for. Changes and improvements were soon made at the big house and its gardens. Electric light was installed; new plant houses were built, for the Duchess loved flowers, especially orchids and other exotics; overgrown shrubs were cleared to open views; new cottages were planned for the estate. Already a well-known hostess in society, the Duchess made the Deepdene the scene of brilliant entertainment. Royalty and nobility were among her many friends who included members of the Marlborough family with whom she remained on good terms. Her young nephew by marriage, Winston Churchill, whom the Duchess and Lord William had assisted in his career, later wrote: "They bade me visit them continuously . . . . thus I paid frequent visits to Deepdene with its comfort and splendour".

News that the wealthy American widowed Duchess (who wished to be known as Lily, fearing Lilian would be rhymed with million), had taken a lease of the Deepdene had aroused considerable interest among Dorking townspeople. She quickly established a happy relationship with them and retained a warm place in their affections throughout her life. On her marriage to Lord William Beresford in April 1895, little more than a year after she came to Dorking, local people "subscribed handsomely" for a wedding present, a "beautiful pair of silver candelabra." Kind-hearted and generous, she identified herself in many ways with the life of the town and there were few institutions which did not benefit from her wealth and hospitality. The Cottage Hospital was a favourite charity. She visited it regularly, gave presents to its patients, took an active part in its management and finally endowed it with £1000 in memory of her late husband, Lord William Beresford. Generous subscriptions and gifts were given to the workhouse, Albany House home for poor girls,

Canon Chichester outside the Vicarage, a photograph taken c1915.

Wall monument in opus sectile *by James Powell & Sons to Lily, Duchess of Marlborough (1855-1909), in the south aisle.*

and the Boys Brigade. To the Literary Institute she gave £100 and "a fine collection of books". The National Schools received £100 towards the building fund. Local societies were not overlooked. To the Dorking and District Angling Society she gave exclusive fishing rights on a mile stretch of the River Mole, stipulating only that its members each pay one shilling annually to the Cottage Hospital. As president of the Rifle Club she donated several handsome prizes. The Brockham Rose Association held an exhibition at the Deepdene at her invitation; perhaps its members were shown the newly planted William Allen Richardson roses. The recently formed Dorking Urban District Council received timely help. Informed of difficulties in finding suitable offices, the Duchess built premises in South Street (at the corner of Junction Road) and leased part of them to the Council and part for use as a Post Office.

But the chief beneficiary of the Duchess's generosity was her own church, St. Martin's parish church, to which she gave "with a lavish hand". She defrayed a large portion of the cost of installing electric light and the whole cost (£200) of thoroughly cleaning and renovating the interior. Brass ornaments and the chancel gates were re-lacquered or re-gilded at her expense. A substantial sum was given for improvements to the organ, including the addition of several stops and the vox humana. Perhaps it was this which prompted the organist, Edward Withers, to dedicate to Her Grace his own setting, in the key of G, of the office of Holy Communion. As one writer put it: "What the church owes to her will never be known in its entirety", for her giving was unobtrusive and she sought no publicity.

The music of the church service appealed particularly to the music-loving Duchess. She often attended choir practices and twice a year the choir was entertained at the Deepdene. On other occasions choir and church members went on outings further afield at her expense. Her concern for the young choristers, to whom she is reputed to have given useful hints on elocution, is illustrated by a story still told. A sudden rain storm occurred during choir practice and the Duchess, realising some of the children were ill-equipped for the weather, sent for protective clothing for those who needed it.

The Duchess's fondness for children was well known in the town. She would frequently stop to admire babies in their prams during her walks and would even on occasion ask the mother's permission to kiss them. The treats at the Deepdene for children from all the elementary schools were red letter days in their lives and perhaps gave equal pleasure to their kind hostess.

News of the Duchess's serious illness in 1908 caused concern, and bulletins were posted at the principal gate of the Deepdene. On her death on 11 January 1909 the whole town seems to have been genuinely grief-stricken and signs of mourning were everywhere. After a short service conducted in the great hall of the Deepdene by the Revd. B. S. Phillips, the coffin, followed by a long procession of mourners, was taken to Dorking station on its way to Golders Green where the Duchess was cremated. Her ashes were taken to Ireland and laid beside her husband's grave in Clonegam churchyard, Corraghmore. A memorial service, conducted by Canon E. A. Chichester, was held at St. Martin's on 18 January and the church bells tolled a muffled peal. The church was crowded and the long list of those present, personal friends, the Deepdene staff and representatives of every organisation and institution with which the Duchess had been connected, filled nearly two columns in the *Dorking Advertiser.* Inside the west door of St. Martin's is a strikingly handsome tablet inscribed: "To the Glory of God and in memory of LILY DUCHESS of MARLBOROUGH of the Deepdene, Dorking, a Benefactress to this church who died 11 January 1909. This memorial is erected by friends and parishioners of Dorking." The Duchess's connection with Dorking is further perpetuated in the names of two streets, Marlborough and Beresford Roads.

Her many unobtrusive kindnesses and her characteristically American spontaneity and generosity have become almost a legend, and older Dorking residents can still recall tales they heard from their mothers of visits to the Deepdene and of the kindly lady who lived there. In the words of the obituary in the *Dorking Advertiser,* hers was "A Whole Life Well-Spent".

Chapter 5
Music at St. Martin's

Our knowledge of the music in St. Martin's church in the early 19th century comes from A. J. B. Beresford Hope's book, *Worship in the Church of England*, 1874. Beresford Hope (1820-87) was the youngest son of Thomas Hope whose Dorking home was the Deepdene. He vividly described his childhood experiences in the medieval parish church where there was 'a decrepit western gallery for the band' which was made up of an 'unruly gang of volunteers, with fiddles and wind instruments'. Legend has it that the congregation gave one of these players the nickname of 'Sound your A-Dawes', because of the frequent stage whispers heard during the service appealing to him to give the key note on his instrument. Each Sunday there was a rendering of a psalm in the Tate and Brady metrical version of 1696 which was known as the 'New Version'. (The 'Old Version' was by Sternold and Hopkins 1560.)

Beresford Hope remembered with approval the purchase of an organ which was recorded in the minutes of a special vestry meeting called in January 1831. It cost £500. (For the history of the organ *see* Chapter 3). At the same meeting the appointment was recorded of the first organist, Mr. Edward James Richard Russell at a salary of £40 per year, who seems to have negotiated the purchase and received a commission of £20 from Elliot and Hill, the organ builders.

According to Edward Russell's death certificate, he was born in Guildford probably in 1795. Nothing is known so far of his career before he came to Dorking in 1831. The census of 1841 records that he was living, married and with a family, in Back Lane (now Church St). By the 1851 census he is called Professor of Music and living at Mount House. In 1861 he is recorded as living in East Street (now High St). Russell resigned the post of organist about 1865 and died on 25 November 1871. The funeral service was conducted by the vicar, the Revd. Philip Hoste, in St. Martin's, and he is buried in the Reigate Road cemetery. His son, William, who was born in 1846, was ordained and eventually became Precentor of St. Paul's Cathedral, London where, in collaboration with John Stainer, he produced the 1875 Cathedral Psalter, a milestone in congregational psalm singing.

Nine years after Russell was appointed as the organist of St. Martin's a fifteen year old youth was sent by his father to Dorking to be coached by the vicar, the Revd. James Joyce. The 1841 census lists four or five people resident in the vicarage and described as 'pupil'. Unfortunately the name Frederick Gore Ouseley is not recorded at that date. Frederick's father, Sir Gore Ouseley, was a high-ranking diplomat, who had been British Ambassador to Persia. He was interested in music and was one of the founders of the Royal Academy of Music. Frederick was a child prodigy who played duets with the Princess Victoria. He remained in Dorking for three years and during this time he became a firm friend of James Joyce's eldest son, James Wayland (1812-87), who at this period was a curate to his father. The two young men shared musical interests and Frederick, according to the biography written in 1896 by F. W. Joyce, the son of James Wayland, had installed a one manual chamber organ built in 1790 by John Avery, a notable organ builder of the 18th century, in the loft of the vicarage stables (the present vicarage). Frederick succeeded to the baronetcy on the death of his father in 1844. He was destined to become Professor of Music at Oxford and precentor of Hereford Cathedral in 1856.

His greatest contribution to the music of the Anglican church was the establishment of the College of St. Michael, Tenbury, in 1856, of which he became the Warden. This was a mid-19th century attempt to reform and raise the standards of Cathedral music. James Wayland Joyce, who was the incumbent at Burford, Salop, nearby, laid the foundation stone of the College and became its first fellow. The foundation of St. Michael's College followed a difficult period for Ouseley. He had been ordained deacon in 1849, and became curate at the new church of St. Barnabas, Pimlico, where his specific task was the formation of a choir. This he did and both presented the organ and financed the choir. The Tractarian ritual at the church, however, aroused the attention of a mob who chanted 'no popery'. These troubles, known as the Pimlico riots, rose to a climax on Sunday 17 November 1850 when the church was guarded during services by 100 policemen.

The sensitive Ouseley resigned and did not proceed to ordination as a priest until 1855. The choir was left in the hands of the Revd. Henry Fyffe, a colleague. In the search for a new home, it seems that Dorking was considered, a tantalising might-have-been, before Tenbury was finally settled upon. Certainly Ouseley had a continuing influence on the music at St. Martin's until his sudden death in 1889, and it is interesting to note that the rebuilding of St. Martin's from 1866 was undertaken by the same architect, Henry Woodyer, who had designed the College of St. Michael. It is most probable that Ouseley gave his expert opinion on the rebuilding of the organ in 1868. He played at the rededication of the chancel in that year and gave the two foot stop on the Choir Organ. Perhaps there was an awkward time in the relationship from 1877, when he appears to have been responsible for encouraging the newly appointed Dorking organist, Langdon Colborne, to move to Hereford Cathedral (*see* below). Ouseley's compositions, anthems, hymn tunes and psalm chants, still feature in the music of St. Martin's today.

After Russell left, the next musician of interest at St. Martin's was Ernest Augustus Sydenham, who was born at Shepton Beauchamp in Somerset on 5 October 1847. He appears to have received his training at the Royal Conservatorium in Leipzig. The standard of English musical academies at that time was poor and many of our country's finest musicians chose to receive a training abroad. Sydenham came to Dorking as the organist of St. Martin's in 1869 not long after the building of the Forman chancel. In the 1871 census he was lodging in Horsham Road, an address which he retained throughout the four years of this tenure. He married Miss May Ann Cooke on 28 July 1872 in St. Martin's and their first child, Ethel May, was christened by the Revd. Philip Hoste on 11 June 1873. It would appear that Sydenham founded the Dorking Amateur Musical Society in 1872. On 24 August 1873 Sydenham became organist of Farnham parish church where in 1875, Philip Hoste became Rector. After seven years there he took up the appointment of organist at All Saints Church, Scarborough, and died in 1891. A number of his anthems were published by Novello.

After Sydenham left there was a period of four years during which four organists served St. Martin's. The longest serving of the four was Mr. George H. Hughes who was appointed in February 1874. He came to Dorking from Worcester where he had been Assistant Organist of the Cathedral and organist of St. Bee's Theological College. Hughes officiated at the dedication of the new nave on St. Barnabas Day 11 June 1874. In common with many other important parish churches in this country who adopted the tractarian and ecclesiological practices, St. Martin's copied the musical practices of the cathedrals: an all male surpliced choir who sang canticles in the offices to settings and in addition frequently sang an anthem, particularly at evensong. The music lists appeared every month in the Parish Magazine from the inception of that journal in 1872. In July 1874 besides the hymns and organ voluntaries, Wesley in F, (both Morning and Evening Canticles), Barnby in D (Te Deum), Spark in D (Evening Canticles) were sung by the choir. The records show that on 18 April 1875 a son, George Cumberland, was baptised and that George and Edith Hughes were living in Vincent Road.

George Hughes's departure is not noted in the Parish Magazines for 1877 but he must have left by July when the appointment of Langdon Colborne appeared in the Magazine. Langdon Colborne, according to John Ebenezer West's *Cathedral Organists*, was born in Hackney in September 1835. He was a pupil of George Cooper, sub-organist of St. Paul's Cathedral. From 1860 when he was appointed organist of St. Michael's College, Tenbury, in succession to John Stainer, he had constant connections with the Revd. Sir F. Gore Ouseley. From Tenbury he proceeded to Beverley Minster in 1874. He came to Dorking from Wigan parish church in July 1877 but had hardly arrived when, in August, Townsend Smith the organist of Hereford Cathedral died. At the end of September Colborne left Dorking for Hereford where he remained until his death in September 1889, six months after the illustrious Precentor, Frederick Gore Ouseley. The Archbishop of Canterbury awarded him the degree of Doctor of Music in 1883.

At the beginning of December 1877 Edward Withers was appointed organist and choirmaster to St. Martin's. Withers was born on 29 December 1855, the son of a cabinet maker of the same name at Middlebridge, Romsey, Hampshire. How he received his training as a musician we do not know. One source states that he was an articled pupil to Dr. Prendegast, organist and Master of the Choristers at Winchester Cathedral. This would seem probable since it was a common Victorian practice. The records of Romsey Abbey show him to be organist there in 1876 when according to the churchwardens' accounts he was paid the sum of £30 per annum. The January issue of St. Martin's Parish Magazine for the year 1878 compliments him on the high standard of the music over the Christmas Festival in 1877. The Parish Magazines in the years between 1878 and 1899 show the steady broadening of the choir's repertoire. It is interesting to note that in the July issue of the magazine for 1878 attention is drawn to the problem of choir recruitment because of the late hour of the weekly practice — 8.15 p.m. on a Tuesday. This was due to the hour of closure of most business houses in Dorking — 8.00 p.m!

Withers demanded high standards — the choir was taken to London on 23 September 1897 to attend the services at St. Paul's Cathedral and Westminster Abbey. Evidently the aim was to broaden their horizons and introduce them to the proper performance of church music in those places of worship. 36 boys and men travelled at the cost of £8.6s.9d.

By 21 September 1880 St. Martin's was using *Hymns Ancient and Modern* (1875 edition) and the *Westminster Abbey Chant Book*. The actual Psalter is not mentioned. From the churchwardens' accounts of 30 April 1882 we gather that the organist was paid the sum of £80 per annum.

The Parish Magazine for June 1884 reported a Diocesan Choral Festival at Winchester Cathedral with a total of 1,500 voices. St. Martin's choir numbering 35 attended and one of the festival conductors was Edward Withers. The South Eastern Railway Company advertised a special train and reduced fares.

By 1885 Withers was well established as a musician in Dorking. It was about this time that he married and settled at 6, Vincent Road where he stayed for the rest of his life. On 16 November 1889 Rupert, a son of Edward and Charlotte Maria Withers, was baptised by the Revd. Edward Chichester. The partnership of Chichester as vicar and Withers as organist was to continue until the former's retirement in 1921.

Both in the town and in the Deanery Withers demonstrated his musical leadership. In the earliest days, the Deanery Festivals coincided with the Patronal Festival at St. Martin's. In 1889 there was a performance of Mendelssohn's 'Lobesang' (The Hymn of Praise) and in 1890 two performances on 4 July of 'The Prodigal Son' by Arthur Sullivan were held in St. Martin's. The Dorking Choral Society, formed out of the former Amateur Musical Society or Choral Class, listed amongst its performances under Withers's baton in those final years of the 19th century Handel's 'Messiah' and 'Judas Maccabeus', Sullivan's 'The Golden Legend', Mendelssohn's 'Elijah' and 'St. Paul'.

The choir of St. Martin's frequently performed selections from Handel's 'Messiah' on Easter Day, repeated on Low Sunday, as well as Spohr's 'Last Judgement' (Advent 1890). The weekly music lists were of cathedral-like proportions:

Te Deum: Woodward in E flat, Arnold in C, Garrett in F, Stanford in B flat, Withers in E etc.

Magnificat and Nunc Dimittis: Garrett in F, Garrett in D, Stainer in E, Wesley in F etc.

Anthems: Ascribe unto the Lord and Blessed be the God and Father — Wesley; O where small wisdom be found — Boyce; Cry aloud and shout — Croft; Remember now thy Creator — Steggall etc.

Withers wrote a setting for the communion service dedicated to Lily, Duchess of Marlborough who was a great champion in the cause of music at St. Martin's between 1894 and 1909. The programme of an organ recital which he gave on 20 February 1895 demonstrates the musical taste of the period:

Sonata No. 2 — Mendelssohn; Berceuse — Spinney; Oh had I Jubal's lyre — Handel; Fugue in E minor — Bach; Pastorale — [W.T.] Best; Toccata — [Theodore] Dubois; Andante in F sharp minor — Wesley; Offertoire in D — Batiste.

The membership of the choir was obviously regarded an honour to be prized so that each boy was given an ornate certificate to commemorate his entry into the noble band of singers with Canon Chichester's signature upon it.

J.A. Howard recalls Edward Withers as a personality.

"I served as a choirboy under Edward Withers from 1914 — 1918, these were the years of the first world war.

We were expected to attend choir practice in the (old) church room after school from 4.30 to 5 on four afternoons a week. Mr. Withers was known to us boys as 'Teddy' (but not in his hearing). The usual routine at these practices was that 'Teddy' would pick on a boy to sing several verses of Psalms, after this we would combine and sing the hymns for the following Sunday. Thursday evening with the full quire of men and boys we would practise the psalms, hymns and an anthem.

Teddy was a strict disciplinarian. If he found a boy misbehaving during the service he would step down and administer a sharp slap to the head with a book.

We choir boys were paid half a crown on first joining (which was payment for a quarter). As we progressed in Teddy's estimation we moved up towards the front, our goal was to reach one of the four separate stalls nearest to the screen (now of course removed). Every so often our progress would be reviewed and our money increased. I believe the top boy received one pound for a quarter. A register was kept of attendances at practices and absences noted at the end of each quarter and sometimes a fine would be imposed.

Teddy had several pupils who were learning to play the organ. He would ask one of us choirboys to help occasionally. At that time the organ console was attached to the organ direct and I believe run by water. However just inside the vestry there was a long wooden arm which when pumped up and down filled the bellows. A small lead weight on a length of string had to be kept towards the top showing a good pressure of air was maintained. I remember if pumping was not maintained at a regular rate, there would be a bang from the console and a sharp word to 'wake up'. We received a shilling for about nearly an hour's labour.

We practised several songs for some weeks. I can only remember 'The Ash Grove' and 'Loch Lomond' among others which we sang at a Freemasons' dinner held at the old Red Lion Hotel. We were given a meal and a small gratuity.

Mr. Withers had two sons. I still remember the evening full choir practice when he had that day received news that his son had been killed, it shocked many of us boys to see our Teddy actually in tears. His other son played the cello and lived on in Dorking for several years. He married a Miss Davey whose father was a well known figure and had a business in the High Street. They moved away after several years.

I recall that the midday eucharist service was sometimes sung to a setting composed by Edward Withers''.

It is sad that towards the end of his half century as organist of St. Martin's the congregation complained about the endless repetition of the same settings of the canticles and the anthems. He died on 20 October 1927 at his home in Vincent Road of a cerebal haemorrhage in the presence of his son Rupert. The great attendance at his funeral (22 October) bears witness to his stature in the town. His widow was given the proceeds of a fund which had been set up to celebrate his 50 years of devoted service to St. Martin's church.

Following the death of Edward Withers, Cyril Knight was appointed organist and choirmaster. Knight remained in the post for two and a half years before, in the late summer of 1930, he was appointed to a similar position at St. Mary's church, Primrose Hill, London. Later in life he became organist and choirmaster of St. Stephen's church, Bournemouth. Whilst at Dorking he worked from an address in London, although he had a relative living in the parish.

In 1930 William Cole was the organist of Leyton parish church when he applied for the post at Primrose Hill. The vicar at St. Mary's informed Cole that he had filled the post but that Dorking parish church would be in need of a new organist. In October 1930 Mr. William Cole, F.R.C.O. L.R.A.M., a young man of twenty one, began a musical connection with our town which was to continue for forty seven years. In the previous year Ralph Vaughan Williams, the composer, who had been associated with the area since his childhood, and his wife, Adeline, moved into the parish, to a house off the Westcott Road called 'White Gates'. It was a convenient house for Adeline because she never enjoyed good health. Ralph Vaughan Williams had been the conductor of the Leith Hill Musical Festival since its foundation in 1905. The Festival was made up of choirs from the towns and villages within a radius of ten miles of Abinger Hall and soon William Cole was involved. When Ralph Vaughan Williams gave up the conductorship in 1953 William Cole took up the baton the following year, retiring in 1977.

The influence of Ralph Vaughan Williams began to be felt in St. Martin's where, for instance in 1947, the Sunday nearest the great man's 75th birthday, 12 October, was marked by the performance of his music in the services. He frequently conducted one group of singers or another in concerts in St. Martin's. During the war years the Festival became the Leith Hill Festival Choir and between 1941, when the Dorking Halls were taken over by the Government, and 1947 all the recitals were held in the church.

Much could be written about the twenty four years during which William Cole was organist. His enthusiasm and high standards endeared him to generations of young choristers, many of whom graduated to the back row. His professionalism and warm hearted personality formed a bridge between choir and congregation. His many musical friends, such as Ruth Dyson, came to perform in the church and enhanced the reputation of St. Martin's Dorking as a place where good music was frequently to be heard.

St. Martin's Dorking has had the privilege of watching William Cole rise in his profession. By 1943 he had gained the D. Mus. Degree from London University, and became a Professor at the Royal Academy of Music. After he left in September 1954 St. Martin's continued to follow him with interest as he took up the post of Secretary to the Associated Board of the Royal Schools of Music and, in 1970, President of the Royal College of Organists. In July 1954 Dr. Cole was appointed by the Chancellor of the Duchy of Lancaster to be organist and Master of Music at the Queen's Chapel of the Savoy. The vicar, Kenneth Evans, said at his leaving party 'St. Martin's, Dorking, between 1929 (sic) and 1954 has had a standard of music as high as any parish church that I know and, much as we rejoice with him in his new appointment, we cannot but be conscious of our loss'.

In October 1954 Mr. D.J. Wilks, B.A. B.Mus. F.R.C.O. a graduate of Durham University and a Limpus Prize winner, took up the post of organist and choirmaster, an arrangement which was to last but a few months before he moved to St. Peter's, Cranley Gardens, London.

In the following September of 1955 Mr. Neil Turner B.A. A.R.C.O., a former chorister and assistant to Dr. Cole, became the organist and choirmaster to be followed in 1961 by Mr. Desmond Swinburn F.R.C.O.

The 1960's were difficult times both within and without church life. Counter attractions from the secular world lured young people away from the choir stalls to rugby and other athletic interests. Dorking was no exception to the rule. In the 1970s St. Martin's became

North-east view of the interior of the church, showing the organ case in the chancel designed by Henry Woodyer in 1868, and the organ case on the east wall of the north aisle, built between 1932 and 1933, a photograph taken c1975.

St. Martin's clergy, choir, organists and servers, including the Vicar, the Revd. Kenneth Evans, and the organist, William Cole, a photograph taken in October 1951 and reproduced, together with a list of the choir, in the programme 'Music for the Re-opening of the Organ', November 1951.

Bronze wall monument to Dr. Ralph Vaughan Williams (1872-1958), designed by David McFall, in the south porch, 1961.

Dr. William Cole at the organ console in the south aisle, a photograph taken c1954.

a Shared Church and that presented certain musical problems. Nevertheless Mr. Swinburn is remembered for his ability as a superb accompanist of both choir and congregation.

The change of emphasis away from mattins to the centrality of the eucharist and the greater participation by the congregation led to the introduction of easy attractive settings of the canticles in the communion by composers such as Patrick Appleford and Martin How. Besides the hymn book, *Ancient and Modern Revised*, 1950, which was introduced in St. Martin's in 1969, the church uses the two supplements, *One Hundred Hymns for Today*, 1969, and *More Hymns for Today*, 1980. The Methodist congregation brought with them the *Methodist Hymn Book* 1933, and *Hymns and Songs*, 1969, and has since adopted the new Methodist book, *Hymns and Psalms*, 1983. At shared services these books are freely interchangeable depending on the clergy in charge for the act of worship.

Following Mr. Swinburn's resignation in late 1976 the choirs of the Methodist and Anglican congregations came closer together under Victor Potter, the Anglican organist and Peter Essex, the Methodist organist. Although they worked separately for their respective services, on many occasions when worship was shared the music was led by an united choir. When Peter Essex found that other commitments prevented him from continuing at the helm of Methodist music, Mr. Alan Pullinger stepped in to fill the gap. Mr. Pullinger was to hold things together during a long interregnum between late 1983 and February 1985 when there was no official Anglican organist. The late Mr. Austin Elder, the able assistant, played for most of the Anglican services during this time.

In February 1985 Miss Rosemary Field was appointed the Anglican organist and choirmaster. Her professional skill and high standards laid the foundations of a strong team of junior choristers whose standards of musicianship and vocal expertise rose rapidly during the eighteen months she was at St. Martin's.

When in the summer of 1986 Miss Field was appointed the sub organist of Birmingham Cathedral, the authorities took the bold step of appointing a single organist and choirmaster for both Anglican and Methodist congregations. Mr. Martin Ellis A.D.C.M., F.R.C.O. (CHM), G.R.S.M., A.R.C.M. was chosen for the post which he took up on 1 September 1986.

Mr. Ellis had been a chorister at the Temple Church under the late Sir George Thalben Ball. In common with Mr. Desmond Swinburn he was an R.J. Pitcher Organ Scholar at the Royal College of Music where he was a pupil of the late Sir John Dykes Bower. After appointments in preparatory schools in Edinburgh and Cheltenham he spent thirteen years as Assistant Director of Music at Taunton School in Somerset. He is a Methodist Local Preacher with experience in both the Anglican and Presbyterian traditions of music and worship. He was a member of the music and general committee that produced the new Methodist hymn book, *Hymns and Psalms*, 1983, and the founder of the British Methodist Youth Choir in 1982 which he directed until 1990. He took up the post of Director of Music at Reigate Grammar School also in September 1986.

Since 1986 the music has widened in style with the advent of a Folk Worship group which is at present in the capable hands of Mr. Peter Essex. Choral evensong is the normal form of worship on the first Sunday evening of each month and on the greater festivals. An anthem is sung every Sunday morning at the 9.30 a.m. parish communion and on many other occasions too. Recitals are arranged during Lent and in the month of November to collect funds for Christian Aid and Crisis at Christmas. In February 1989 the Deanery Festivals of former times were revived under the title of Mole Valley Church Choirs Festival, when 150 singers took part. In 1990 the membership of the combined choir was thirty eight, five of the junior choristers being Bishop's Choristers.

The church between the wars.

S.P.G. Pageant in the Vicarage garden, 1938.

The Revd. George ('Pat') Adams, curate 1910-28.

The Revd. A. Edward Robins, curate 1930-35.

The church between the wars.

St. Martin's Youth Fellowship with the curate, the Revd. John Mortimer, on an Easter Monday outing on Holmbury Hill, c1939.

Canon E. J. Newill, vicar 1927-36.

The Revd. Anthony Weigall, curate 1936-39.

Chapter 6

Kenneth Evans and Jack Roundhill

Kenneth Evans's Time

Kenneth Evans came to St. Martin's in 1949. He had previously been rector of Ockley in this same Deanery and knew the area well. He and Mr. Starey, the retiring incumbent, had been at Clare College, Cambridge, which was then the patron of the Ockley living. Mr. Starey became rector of Ockley in his place. This meant that Kenneth Evans, who had trained at Ripon Hall, Oxford, and who had been ordained deacon in 1938, took on a larger town parish while Mr. Starey took a step towards his retirement, although having been appointed Rural Dean in 1943, he held that office until 1957.

By necessity the war years and those immediately following the war had been a period of 'marking time' in the parish. Despite the upheavals of those times there had not been great changes in the life of St. Martin's. Indeed the shortages and the need to concentrate resources in other ways meant that there had been virtually no work done on the buildings. While, apart from the crack in the tower despite which the bells rang out for victory, there had been no war damage or other disaster, this did not mean that there was not much that needed to be done both in the life of the parish and in the maintenance of buildings.

In 1949 the parish was a much more close-knit community than it is in 1990. The centre of the town was then the centre of population and the move to the outer council estates had not yet begun. Many people commuted to London to work, but the car, the television and the foreign holiday were not yet in the ascendant. Local family ties were stronger and the outlook of the average parishioner was not so cosmopolitan as it was later to become. There was less prosperity and at least as much economic deprivation and the role of the church was clearly recognised as it had been for a hundred years and more.

In St. Martin's there were many fringe members who took no great part in church life, but who regarded themselves as part of the church 'family'. On the other hand there were fewer lay people involved on a day-to-day basis in the life of the parish. Looking at the country as a whole there had been no great upheavals in the Church of England and in many ways the situation was as it had been in 1939.

When Kenneth Evans came to Dorking the parish was staffed by the vicar and one curate, who would have been a young assistant priest in his first or second curacy. In addition the Revd. J.F. Twist, an older man and former curate, was helping and in 1951 Mr. F.N. Doubleday moved back to Dorking, the town of his birth and upbringing. After a distinguished career as a dentist (amongst other distinctions he was honorary dental surgeon at Guy's Hospital), Mr. Doubleday had taken orders on his retirement in 1947. On his return to Dorking he assumed responsibility for Pixham and remained in charge there until forced by ill-health to give up working full-time in 1960. After that Pixham again became the responsibility of one of the curates, though Mr. Doubleday continued to assist until 1969.

With the concentration of the parish and with this level of staffing, visiting by the clergy continued on the old basis of visiting because people were there rather than the modern practice, brought on by shortage of clergy and the distractions of modern life, of visiting only where need is perceived.

The 1950s was the last decade during which the average Church of England parish continued with the traditional pattern of services involving 8 a.m. said communion, 11 a.m. sung mattins and 6.30 p.m. evensong, again with full choir. St. Martin's followed this pattern with in addition a 7 a.m. communion on the first Sunday of the month. There was a sparsely attended communion at 12 noon and, on two Sundays a month, the 11 a.m. service was sung mattins (up to the Benedictus) and sung eucharist. This pattern continued until the end of 1957 when Kenneth Evans wrote in the magazine that 'what is in fact happening is that the greater part of the congregation leave during the hymn following the address'. The PCC discussed the situation and decided with the vicar that on each Sunday there would be sung mattins at 11 a.m. and that on one Sunday a month there would be a family communion at 10 a.m. (later changed to 9.45 a.m.) with music but with no sermon. Kenneth Evans commented that 'it is the first time we have planned a service at which the whole family may worship together early in the day'. The experiment went well and in December 1960 it was decided to have a sung family communion service at 9.45 a.m. each Sunday. The children's church was at the same time and the children came into the service during the offertory hymn. Kenneth wrote that 'it is our aim that this service shall be the central weekly act of worship in St. Martin's'. Mattins continued to be sung at 11 a.m. each Sunday and in addition to the early morning services and evensong, which continued as before, there was once a month a well-attended family service at 3 o'clock on a Sunday afternoon.

Evensong was a different affair from the evening worship of the 1990s. It followed the Book of Common Prayer and a congregation of 200 to 250 was the norm. Many people attended worship twice or even three times on Sunday and it was common then, as it had been since Victorian times, for people to come into church membership as a result of their attendance at evensong. In his later years at St. Martin's, Kenneth Evans, like all other vicars of that period, saw some fall away in support for evensong. This was due to many reasons including the changes in social behaviour and competition from other 'entertainments'. Some saw the final decline as being caused by the "Forsyte Saga" on television! Be that as it may, the numbers attending evensong during Kenneth Evans's time did not drop away as dramatically as they did in some other parishes.

In 1949 and in the years following there were over fifty confirmation candidates each year and still over forty in 1960.

During the 1950s the old streets round the church were cleared and the council estates were built at Goodwyns and Chart Downs. There was a shift of population to the south and many families which had been under St. Martin's wing for generations moved out of its sphere of influence. It is easy to look back and to say that an opportunity was lost, but it was not so easy at the time to realise what was happening or to take steps to deal with the new situation.

Despite these problems Kenneth Evans felt that it was possible to be quite encouraged by the 1950s. There was a flow back into Church of England life and, for instance, figures for communicants went up. Nonetheless this was a time when new ideas for worship and for parish life were being developed. Rome was ready for reform and the Church of England and non-conformist churches, which fifty years before had barely been on speaking terms, were starting to look for ways of co-operation previously unknown. A new phase in the life of the church was to follow.

When Kenneth Evans came to Dorking there was not a lot of money about within St. Martin's. Finance was on a hand-to-mouth basis. The Easter offering was important to the vicar and the Whitsun offering to the curate. Kenneth and Margaret were not at all well off. They did not have a car as they could not afford one. Margaret remembers him bicycling along the High Street under an umbrella and also recalls that people were shocked because in a heatwave she was seen walking along Dorking High Street with no stockings on!

During the years when Kenneth Evans was vicar little change was seen in the church buildings and such funds as were available were used for routine maintenance. In his early years the major fund-raising was to repair the tower so that the bells could once again be rung. Kenneth recalls that when they were rung again there were complaints from those living nearby. However after six months the bells were accepted and there was no more trouble.

When the Evans family moved into the vicarage they found that they had 29 rooms, extensive cellars, and the stabling which has been converted into the present vicarage. The house was in a very poor state and after six years of struggle there was in 1955 a major reconstruction. At that time there was a big Victorian addition at the back which served as a 'Hall' for meetings. This was pulled down and the house in effect returned to the Georgian house it had been before it became a vicarage. The well-known architect Donald McMorran, who was responsible for the church buildings, was in charge. He lived in Dorking and worshipped at St. Martin's. The house was a much more comfortable place to live in after the work was done and it continued to be very much the centre of parish activity.

Pixham church also showed little change in this period and continued to serve its local community. Ranmore was formally linked with St. Martin's in 1950 and Kenneth Evans became the rector, with one of the curates acting as priest-in-charge. (*See* Chapters 8 and 9). The church halls and the verger's cottage opposite Stane House (now re-named Church Court) were largely as they were in pre-war days. They were felt to be adequate for their respective purposes and little money was spent on them.

In 1953 Lord Ashcombe gave the site in Ashcombe Road on which the present Ranmore parsonage house was then built. Mr. McMorran was again the architect. The parish also owned the house 'Mayfield' in London Road, so that there was now good accommodation for two married curates.

Kenneth Evans was assisted by a series of curates, who then moved with the benefit of his training to take on, either straight away or later, parishes of their own. The key lay figure in St. Martin's during Kenneth Evans's time was Stanley Pickford. He was churchwarden. There was nothing he did not know about St. Martin's and quietly and efficiently he removed a load of work from the clergy, allowing them to get on with their real jobs.

Music was of great importance. This is dealt with elsewhere, but the influence of Dr. Cole as organist and choirmaster cannot be ignored when looking at this period. Many would say that he had at St. Martin's a choir that was superior to the then pro-Cathedral choir at Holy Trinity, Guildford. Dr. Cole would not have women in the choir. He wanted the quality of the male voice and, anyway, looked for his boys to turn into adult choristers. Writing in the parish magazine in 1951 Dr. Cole said that "actually, a boy is not a great deal of use until he has been in the choir for two years". He was then seeking more boys aged eight to ten, despite there being already 22 boys in the choir at that time. Much use was made of Vaughan Williams's settings and, following his tradition, the Dorking Bach Choir came to St. Martin's each year to sing the St. John Passion. Dr. Cole left in 1954 and it was by no means easy to keep up the standards he had set. The connection with Dr. Vaughan Williams was commemorated when, on 16 June 1961, a plaque in his memory was unveiled in the south porch.

Sunday schools flourished under Kenneth Evans. This did not just happen and much work was put in by clergy and laity. The prime mover was Dulcie Pickford, who was Stanley Pickford's daughter. She had a very strong children's church with some 150 to 200 children at its peak. Miss Pickford was supported by others, such as Margaret Wiscombe. Evelyn Gibbs ran a Sunday school in the hut in Nower Road for the children in that area and only gave this up in 1966 after 38 years. By the time Kenneth Evans left the parish the Sunday school was facing the same problems as the services and the music, but nonetheless remained an important influence in the parish.

Also significant in parish life was the Youth Club run by Ron and Margaret Pantrey. Membership was confined to confirmed young people over 14 with confirmation candidates as associate members. There were 60 to 70 members and after a few years a junior section was added. Central to club life was the corporate communion at 8 a.m. on the first Sunday of the month followed by breakfast cooked by eight or ten members who had already attended the 7 a.m. service. The club ran on a shoe-string but still managed a wide variety of activities such as quizzes, games evenings, parties, talks, debates and outings. Drama and sport played important roles as did the annual 'Youth Weekend'. During Advent and Lent part of each club evening was a course of study drawn up by the clergy. Nearly every other Sunday the club attended evensong and for older members this was followed by a discussion group. Of course Ron and Margaret had various helpers over this period including in particular Keith Hunt. By the early 1960s changing social patterns affected the membership, but not the enthusiasm of those who ran the club, and it became an open club.

At this time, as indeed at other times, the Mothers' Union was of considerable influence, both for its members and for the work done to assist the pastoral work of the clergy. Margaret Evans as enrolling member (this position is now known as branch leader) was prominent as were Doreen Brice and Nancy Warner in later years.

Weekly study groups were a feature of parish life and there were other social groups including the Parish Fellowship. There were a number of successful 'Parish Weekends' and in 1956 the Revd. J.B. Phillips, the writer well-known for his book, *Letters to Young*

Churches, came to Dorking and ran a Parish Mission with a sermon every evening and a mission for youth. Harvest suppers and parish bazaars were held in the Martineau Hall at the Dorking Halls. Scouts and Guides were important and Kenneth Evans took great interest in them. Peter Mills ran the Pixham Scouts and Tony Bravery the 10th Dorking Troop. Ethel Clear was in charge of the 9th St. Martin's Guides and Norah Simpson was Brown Owl for the Brownies. In 1951 the Guides celebrated their 21st birthday as a St. Martin's company.

Money needed to run the parish was raised by collections in church, by sales of work, by bazaars and by fetes at the vicarage. For instance late in 1950 there was needed £400 towards the £660 or so required to repair the organ, £80 for church vestments and £150 for heating work. A substantial part of this sum was raised in 1951 by the social committee on behalf of the PCC by a sale of work and by a vicarage fete. A typical jumble sale at this time raised £25 to £30, a gift day would bring in about £135 and a fair or bazaar some £140 to £160. The accounts for 1951 show collections in church at £636 with the then Friends of St. Martin contributing £547. At that time the Friends was an envelope scheme, administered for many years by Miss Burton, and had no other function. In the Parish Magazine for June 1951 it was said to be there "to enable parishioners to make an annual contribution which will not be affected by their being able or unable to attend the services of the church on any particular Sunday". It was mentioned that, while some were able to give £20, "some give two shillings a year".

Total income of the parish in 1951 came to £1,369. With the Diocesan quota at £160 the books just about balanced. In 1954 an extra £1,000 was needed for work to be carried out on the tower and bells and this was raised by similar methods. By 1957 the fair in the autumn was bringing in £250, but the PCC was becoming concerned at the financial instability of the parish and at the lack of a regular income. In 1958 total income was £2,398 with a deficit of £118 and in 1959 income had increased to £3,707 but the deficit on the year had increased to £1,080. Something had to be done and, with the concept of 'Christian Stewardship' becoming fashionable, an American based company was called in to run a stewardship campaign.

The campaign in 1959 did not meet with universal approval, but it was certainly a financial success. With hindsight and with more experience, such things as the chicken and wine meal for 800 in the Dorking Halls, the pressure selling and the public declarations as to amounts of giving were not entirely happy features and have been modified in subsequent campaigns. The company guaranteed a certain result, but there was no need to take up the guarantee. Income was raised to £6,891 in 1960 (the first complete year of working after the campaign) and despite increased expenditure on important items that had previously been deferred, there was a surplus in that year of £1,000. With the benefit of tax recovery on covenants, the parish looked forward to a regular and increasing income. The plan was that there would be no more fairs, fetes or gift days and that there would be no more collections in church. As the years passed things did not quite work out this way. Partly this was because, instead of deciding to have 'renewal' campaigns on a regular basis, the PCC and indeed the parish as a whole felt that it needed a rest from stewardship campaigning.

Throughout Kenneth's time administration continued much as it had in previous years.

At Diocesan and Deanery levels the 'Conferences' were sounding boards rather than decision-making bodies. The building of the new Cathedral was of importance as indicated by frequent references in the Parish Magazine and by the real joy at the consecration in 1961. In the parish the PCC discussed and decided parish affairs under the guidance of the vicar and outside giving was by special collections and events rather than by grant from the PCC. As Chairman, Kenneth Evans had the facility of knowing how people's thoughts were going and many recall him saying "What in fact you are saying is . . .". With a verger to help, the church was kept clean and tidy by voluntary helpers like Miss Cottrell and Miss Spooner. The churchyard remained closed to burials.

During this period ecumenical relations were improving. Kenneth Evans found it a slow start in Dorking. He recognised that, thanks to the Dorking Council of Churches, a Good Friday service, the Week of Prayer for Christian Unity, the Women's World Day of Prayer and Inter-Church Aid for Refugees became features of Dorking church life. Nonetheless he relied much more on personal contacts. In particular he was friendly with the United Reformed Minister, Mr. Follett, who was sadly missed when he died in 1962 as a result of an illness contracted in India when at the Assembly of the World Council of Churches.

Kenneth Evans was Rural Dean of the Dorking Deanery during the latter part of his time as vicar of St. Martin's. In 1963 he was appointed Archdeacon of Dorking and went to live in Guildford. Five years later he was consecrated in Guildford Cathedral as Bishop of Dorking, when this Suffragan appointment was created in the Guildford Diocese. Following this announcement a fund was set up and the parish was delighted to welcome Kenneth and Margaret to parish communion on 20 October 1968 when his episcopal ring was presented to him by a packed congregation. He only retired from this post on his birthday on 7 November 1985. Those who attended the splendid sung eucharist on that day in Guildford Cathedral remember it as a great occasion and probably the only time they will hear a Cathedral organ playing 'Happy Birthday to You'. He remains Assistant Bishop of Guildford.

Kenneth and Margaret were much loved in Dorking. Many remember him looking through the chancel screen and leaning out of the pulpit. His sermons were short, instructive and often intentionally controversial. Kenneth says of the vicarage that it was an impossible house but they enjoyed living there and talks of his 'great years' in Dorking. He feels that in those days in a town such as this you could still be vicar of everybody and that was what he set out to be. Perhaps the world outside was changing more rapidly than those in St. Martin's realised, but certainly Kenneth Evans left the parish in good heart to meet the challenges of the sixties.

Jack Roundhill's Time

Jack Roundhill succeeded Kenneth Evans as vicar of St. Martin's in August 1963. It is never easy to follow someone who has been not only popular but successful in any job, yet Jack gave St. Martin's the leadership it needed.

Born in England, Jack Roundhill was brought up in Northern Ireland and he still retains traces of his Ulster accent. He was educated in Northern Ireland and then went to Trinity College, Dublin, before being ordained. After a curacy in Harrow he went back to Ireland to become chaplain at Queen's University, Belfast, and secretary to the Irish Student

Christian Movement. He then became vicar of St. Paul's, South Harrow, for seven years and after five years as vicar of St. Leonard's, Heston, he arrived in Dorking with his wife, Marion, and their three children and a fourth, Clare, on the way. The family was completed when Liam was born in 1967.

While always willing to give a lead, Jack Roundhill's style was to seek consensus where he could and always to accept the will of the majority. He was by nature a teacher and he was sympathetic to the change that was in the air in the 1960s.

With the war years receding and with technological developments, people's horizons were shifting and widening. This called for a re-assessment of faith within the Church of England and the possibility of changes which only a few years before had been unthinkable. The New English Bible was published in 1961 and the Anglican-Methodist negotiations were going on through the 1960s. The new forms of service came out following the Prayer Book Measure in 1965, which enabled the Church of England to embark lawfully on liturgical reform. The controversial report, *Partners in Ministry*, which criticized the pay and deployment of clergy as wasteful, inadequate and failing to meet contemporary needs, was published in 1967. In the same year work began on the Commission relating to Anglo-Roman Catholic Inter-Communion. On top of this and other 'official' activity, Bishop John Robinson had published *Honest To God* in 1963.

Jack Roundhill viewed all this with an open and enquiring mind. (He has written several booklets on different sects, particularly Jehovah's Witnesses and the Mormons). He welcomed the opportunity to express our faith in modern terms. This was shown at once by his revised style in the Parish Magazine with its 'modern' format and covers and in particular by his monthly column, 'Daybook of a Vicar', which educated and informed his readers, while keeping them amused. On the other hand he was not dogmatic. For instance while he used the New English Bible himself, he did not object to others reading from the Authorised Version. He saw that Kenneth Evans had started the change in services by the introduction of family communion. Jack Roundhill made no secret of his own view that the Lord's Supper on the Lord's Day should have priority. The introduction of new services was debated fully in the parish and in the PCC, which had the final say. In April 1965 it was decided that mattins should no longer be a sung service, save on exceptional occasions, and before long the congregation at that service at 11 a.m. was down to about thirty. Mattins on Sunday finally dropped out of regular use with the introduction of Methodist worship.

After a six month period of experiment and after a comprehensive questionnaire had been widely distributed and completed by 120 members of the congregation, a decision was reached by the PCC as to the use of the new form of communion service then known as 1967 Series II. By this decision, taken in June 1968, it was agreed that, on Sundays, St. Martin's should use the new service on a regular basis, but that the 1662 service should continue to be used at the monthly 7 a.m. service, at the Tuesday morning communion and at Christmas, Easter and Whitsun.

A believer in short sermons, Jack Roundhill used his as opportunities for bringing home not more than one or two points. He found that the parish communion was not ideal for teaching and he looked to evensong for this. He liked to publish the theme of his sermons and he used them to lay out the faith of the church as expressed in the creeds.

As was common in the Church of England at this time, there was a fall in the number of confirmation candidates. In 1968 the number had dropped to 27 and in 1975 the figure was 13. Certainly it was true that there was a much higher percentage of candidates who had decided to come forward themselves, as opposed to those who came because of parental or other pressure.

The church building itself was badly in need of attention. This had been recognised for some years and had been one of the spurs behind the 1959 stewardship campaign. There were no major structural faults, but it needed a thorough clean and re-decoration inside. Many people including Jack Roundhill felt that the chancel screen divided priest from people and should be removed. The Diocesan Advisory Committee did not agree at first, but with the backing of the views of the Bishop of Guildford, which had been expressed at the vicar's induction service in 1963, this proposal was finally accepted.

Other major changes were debated in order to bring the priest and people closer, including re-arranging the chancel, moving the choir and re-siting and lowering both pulpit and font and providing further vestry accommodation, but none of these suggestions were put into effect. In 1965 the agreed work was carried out under the direction of Jim Ralph, who had taken over as church architect, and under the guidance of Dick Knott, who was chairman of the buildings committee. This resulted in the cleaning and redecorating of the walls of the nave and chancel, the carpeting of the chancel, the removal of the screen (the cross is still stored in the crypt), the cleaning and lightening of the panelled wooden chancel roof and the introduction of new lighting there. The seven red sanctuary lamps were reduced to a single central lamp. Sadly, on grounds of cost, no new lighting was introduced into the nave, although the hanging lamps were modified. The south door and porch were left as they were. Access for the disabled was not a live issue at that time and if it had been much later heartache and expense might have been saved!

This was the only major work on the church itself needed in Jack Roundhill's time until it was found in the early 1970s that the stonework on the tower and spire was unsafe and the PCC was told that it would cost some £9,000 to repair. In those days this was a very large sum of money and it was typical of the social conscience of the time that there was a strong faction within the PCC favouring the removal of Dorking's premier land-mark and symbol of our faith, if this would release funds then and in the future to go to help those in need outside these shores. The tower and spire were reprieved when individual donations were received to pay for the work on the four pinnacles and the PCC decided to have the necessary repairs done. It is good to see in the ringing chamber the board giving details of the peal rung in 1974 to commemorate the 100th anniversary of the building of the church.

In 1972 to mark the centenary of the birth of Dr. Ralph Vaughan Williams, Marion Roundhill organised a working party which resulted in the making of the kneelers for the Lady Chapel. Each features a different aspect of Vaughan Williams's work and each was designed by the person who worked it. The furniture for the Lady Chapel had been renewed at the time of the re-decoration of the church. The organ was, as it always is, an expensive item. In 1970 an estimate was obtained for over £2,000 for necessary work. A move within the PCC to obtain an electronic organ was resisted and, under the guidance of Norman Gibbs, the money needed was raised by subscription and the work carried out. In 1972

View from the chancel looking west, during the alterations when the chancel screen was removed, a photograph taken July 1965.

The Parish Conference at Netley House, Gomshall, 1971.

after the death of Jim Hunter his widow, Eileen, gave the aumbry and the central light was hung in the Lady Chapel.

When Jack and Marion came to Dorking they felt, like Kenneth and Margaret before them, that the vicarage with all its disadvantages was a lovely family house to live in. Not only could it absorb the Roundhills and their five children, but also gave plenty of scope for parish activities in both house and garden. The Roundhills held an annual parish garden party, reviving an earlier tradition. It involved many people and was eagerly looked forward to. Nothing came of suggestions for a new vicarage, one house looked at by the Diocese being Leslie House in Archway Place nearer the church. In addition the plan put forward by the Diocese for conversion of the stables as retired clergy houses came to nothing. The building, now the vicarage, was said to be too close to the Westcott Road!

The debate about the tower and spire typified the growing feeling about the responsibility of the church to the outside world. Nonetheless there was reluctance to grasp the nettle of continuing stewardship. Income from stewardship giving had declined to £6,068 in 1964 with the accounts only just in balance and it was decided to have a renewal campaign in 1966. However when in the next year the financial position improved the campaign was cancelled. Finally in the autumn of 1968 a renewal campaign was mounted. It differed from the 1959 campaign in that it was run by the Diocesan Stewardship Adviser and it did not feature the more aggressive elements previously used. Certainly it stirred the consciences of the laity and caused controversy, probably no bad thing. Nearly 600 families were visited at least twice and many new offers of service were made. The campaign resulted in the income of the PCC rising to over £9,300 in 1969, which was a most welcome increase of some 50%.

It was agreed in the mid 1960s that giving outside the parish should be decided by the PCC. For instance in 1967 the figure for outside giving was £500 and this dropped to £400 in 1968. With the increased income after the stewardship campaign the figure was increased to £1,000 in 1969. By 1975 the principle of giving a percentage of income was established, so as to prevent the temptation only to give away what was left over. In that year outside giving was agreed by the PCC to be 15% of income, which meant £1,700.

It had already been decided in 1967 that it was reasonable even in a stewardship parish to raise funds in addition to stewardship giving. The very fact of doing this was recognised as being a way for members of the congregation to express their stewardship commitment of time and talents. A good example of the result of this decision was the auction in the autumn of 1975 held in the church hall. This involved much hard work, but raised nearly £1,000 towards the £2,700 needed to pay for a new boiler for the church and everyone enjoyed themselves.

During the time that Jack Roundhill was vicar the Church of England was at last making real efforts to improve clergy stipends. In St. Martin's we were helped by the gift made many years previously in the will of the late George White which provided that, on the death of his widow, the churchwardens could pay expenses for the clergy beyond those met by the PCC. On Mrs. White's death in 1965, the fund became available for this purpose.

Like Kenneth Evans, Jack Roundhill believed in visiting as a essential part of his job and also as a help in getting the measure of a community. In those days fewer women went out to work and, in particular in his earlier years in St. Martin's when he had two curates, he indulged in 'blanket' visiting of areas like Parkway and Fairfield Drive. He was keen to minister to as many people as he could and saw this as one way. Another was a number of 'Parish Conferences' which included three residential weekends out of Dorking (two at Grafham and one at Gomshall). These conferences, whether in Dorking or not, all had a teaching theme and helped people to get to know more about each other and the church and also about themselves. They also helped the vicar to find out what made St. Martin's tick.

Throughout Jack Roundhill's time there was an increase in lay activity in the worship of the church and in parish life generally. This was something he very much welcomed and encouraged. He was supported by a number of curates over the years including Roger Hawkins, who followed him from Heston. Three who are well remembered and who have become vicars in this diocese are Norman Kelly, Colin Tickner and David Williams. The laity who worked hard for St. Martin's included those who had been prominent in the time of Kenneth Evans such as John Attlee, Jim Hunter, Robert Grant, Tim Healey, Ron and Margaret Pantrey and, of course, Stanley Pickford until his retirement in 1966 and other churchwardens such as Frank Hunt, Ken Weller and Norman Gibbs. Then there was the new generation with a somewhat different social conscience and set of values typified by June and Michael Day, Judy Wade, Ted Clark and Pam and George Hunter, the last affectionately remembered by the Roundhills as the grit in the oyster when difficult problems were being decided!

Norman Gibbs became in Jack Roundhill's time the upholder of the conservative tradition in church affairs in times of change and it must be said that his excellent relationship with Jack Arthur, whose firm did so much work in the church during these years, was of great benefit to St. Martin's. Jack Roundhill, having read this chapter, writes that, for the record, it should be stated that 'Brian Carr was an important figure in helping the parish to appreciate the need for necessary change during my period at St. Martin's. Norman Gibbs, admittedly, had an important function in the conservative direction and this is rightly mentioned. There was great value in having the two complementary standpoints'.

In the church itself, until her death in 1970, Miss Cottrell was still always there to clean, to open and close and to say the responses in weekday services, when no-one else but the vicar ws there. In addition there was Miss Spooner and other helpers and throughout this period there was a verger in the cottage to keep an eye on the church and churchyard. Walter Chitty as sacristan up to his death in 1975 and Jim Chitty and the other servers were, as ever, a faithful help to the vicar.

Throughout the time when Jack Roundhill was at St. Martin's, Desmond Swinburn was organist and choirmaster. It must be said that Jack was no musician and music was not the important adjunct to worship which it had been in the days of Dr. Cole. The choir was smaller and it became increasingly difficult to recruit boys, but there were still no women or girls. One highly successful artistic event in 1975 was the Youth Festival in the summer with musical and other competitions. This led directly to the formation of the St. Martin's Youth Orchestra with Chris Pratt as its first conductor. There were concerts in the church from time to time and Julian Armitage-Smith provided the funds to enable the front pews to be made removable so that larger orchestras could more conveniently be accommodated.

Sunday schools continued under Dulcie Pickford until her retirement in 1966 and later under Margaret Millard and other helpers. Jack Roundhill did not see the role of the Sunday school as being of the same significance as did Kenneth Evans. He felt that it was of more importance to integrate young people into the family communion and attendance at Sunday school dropped.

Although strenuous efforts were made to maintain continuity, by the end of the 1960s the Scouts no longer met at St. Martin's and Pixham and the numbers attending the different youth organisations which were running from time to time fluctuated. It was no longer realistic to consider running a closed club and the activities which had in past years satisfied club members no longer did so. Social needs and the outlook of young people had changed. There were excellent leaders like Gerald Cooper and his sister Liz, George Hunter, and Boris Kay, but results were less obvious and success was harder to achieve.

Guides and Brownies, still led by Ethel Clear and Norah Simpson respectively, flourished as before. Other church organisations such as the men's working party continued. The OAPs met in the church halls once a week and for the younger adults, under the auspices of the church, the Roundhills supported the Evening Group, the Young Wives and the Supper Club.

The Mothers' Union continued as an important part of church life. Beryl Stedman and Norah Vernon were hard-working branch leaders. There was controversy as to the introduction of divorced people and this was finally allowed in 1974.

St. Barnabas, Ranmore, and Pixham church were served by the clergy from St. Martin's. Ranmore owed much to the Cubitt connection and through Lord Ashcombe funds were found for its upkeep. It kept strictly to the traditional Anglican services. Pixham had the benefit also of the care of Mr. Doubleday who, to use Jack Roundhill's words, 'looked after it like a mother hen' until his retirement in 1969. By the late 1960s there was even talk of closure of both these churches with their small congregations in accordance with what then seemed to be the best use of resources. Fortunately in neither case was the matter pressed. (*See* also Chapters 8 and 9).

During the 1960s substantial essential work was carried out to the church halls, for instance the floor of the main hall had to be replaced and the central heating system overhauled, but otherwise expenditure was kept to a minimum. The verger's cottage fronting Church Street was re-wired in 1964 but was in general need of modernisation. Mayfield, the second curate's house in London Road, became redundant for parish purposes when, in the early 1970s, it was clear that St. Martin's could no longer expect to have a second curate. The house required money to be spent on it and it was sold.

Outside the parish the affairs of the diocese and cathedral did not greatly impinge on St. Martin's, but the ecumenical movement became a leading concern of all denominations. The Dorking Council of Churches and the Ministers' Fraternal were, in Jack Roundhill's words, 'important in the life of the Church'. He recalls with particular pleasure the co-operation of the Baptist Church, but felt that 'ecumenical things never got very far'. Much depended, in his view, on the individual relationships of the local church leaders.

St. Martin's, however, became involved at this time in one major ecumenical project. The high-level talks between Anglicans and Methodists, which could have led to union between their churches, finally came to nothing with the General Synod vote in May

1972, but Dorking had been moving ahead before that. The Methodists in the town had been engaged in separate talks with the United Reformed Church in West Street with a view to forming a United Free Church. For a year from October 1969 the two churches had spent considerable time discussing this local proposal, but in the end the URC Congregational Meeting gave a negative vote.

Jack Roundhill had contemplated this possibility and had discussed the position with the PCC. As a result he was able to call on Ronald Rawlings, the Methodist minister, the next morning and to say "How about a union with St. Martin's?". Mr. Rawlings and Mr. Roundhill had much in common and this was an enormous help in bringing the two congregations together. In December 1971 the PCC agreed to proceed with plans for a shared Anglican-Methodist Church. These plans marked the 25th anniversary of the vicar's ordination. It was a remarkably smooth progress and caused few problems on the Anglican side. With the move from South Street, the sale of their beloved church and the problems of worshipping in strange 'Anglican' surroundings, the difficulties were much greater for the Methodists. Careful negotiation and much hard work and prayer resulted in the Sharing Agreement dedicated at a splendid joint service on 17 June 1973.

This is not the place to seek to assess the success or failure of the venture. The feeling in the two churches at the time was that we had gone about as far as we reasonably could; the two main areas left for future discussion being joint worship and joint finance. From the Anglican side a cause for some regret was the loss of a regular evensong and the attempts in the early years to work out a form of joint service, the so-called Blue Book, were not found to be really satisfactory. The general pattern of services was as before with the Anglican parish communion at 9.30 a.m., the Methodist worship replacing mattins at 11.00 a.m. and joint worship replacing evensong at 6.30 p.m. From the start there was a joint communion service about every quarter. What was really splendid was the close and friendly working relationship between priest, curate and minister and between the two congregations. Many new and lasting friendships were made. (*See* also Chapter 7).

Two important further results from the arrangement with the Methodists were the changes in relation to the church halls and the crypt. These were both planned while Jack Roundhill was vicar, but one was completed after he had left. The possibility of Dorking having an Ecumenical Centre had been talked about in the Dorking Council of Churches but no progress had been found possible. Now the Methodists were selling their church site and were in a position to spend some part of the money locally, while the Anglican church halls were in great need of modernisation. As a result it was agreed that the Methodists should try and become the freehold owners of the halls, which would be rebuilt or developed so as to provide a centre for christian outreach in Dorking under a formal agreement with the Dorking Council of Churches.

This was an unique and forward looking proposal, first floated in the PCC by Colin Tickner, the curate. That it all went through so smoothly says a lot about the local effort and prayer, which convinced the higher powers in both churches of the wisdom of the arrangement. After much consideration, in 1975 Robert Potter (the future Surveyor to the fabric of St. Paul's Cathedral) was appointed architect. He produced several exciting plans and it was finally agreed that within our limited budget we should pull down the verger's cottage and the club room and build an entirely new two-storied block onto the existing halls, containing a new entrance leading to a servery and lounge with a set of offices beyond. Upstairs, rooms were provided for an education unit together with a flat for the warden. The main hall of the former building was transformed when the windows were lowered and a suspended ceiling put in. A new kitchen completed the efficient facilities soon to be in demand by local organisations. It was opened with a service of dedication on 18 September 1977. Despite gloomy prognostications about another 'white elephant' in the local paper, the Christian Centre, as it was to be called, was a success from the start.

Beneath the Methodist church in South Street was an extensive cellar and in this was an open youth club know as the 'Cellar Club'. This made the Anglicans look at the space beneath the church, which was used for storage. Jim Ralph was asked to produce plans and by lowering the floor level of the medieval church by a few inches it was found possible to provide a good area for youth work. The items for storage such as the Guide equipment were moved to the vicarage stables and work was put in hand. Much hard labour was put in by members of the club and by members of both congregations and this meant that the cost of the work was kept to a minimum. The result was that the club, renamed the 'Crypt Club', was able to move to St. Martin's and open in January 1976, with Bernie Fishlock as its leader.

Like Kenneth Evans before him, Jack Roundhill was Rural Dean of the Dorking Deanery during his latter years in Dorking. The Deanery Synod was, like its predecessor the Ruridecanal Conference, little more than a talking-shop, but he found his role to be important pastorally as leader of the Deanery clergy. Shortly before he left St. Martin's at the end of February 1976 Jack Roundhill was appointed a Canon at Guildford Cathedral. In making that appointment the Bishop wrote that it was in recognition of 'the faithful and active work he has done as a Parish Priest' and he also mentioned the work done by Marion in parish and diocese. Jack is not given to looking back — there is so much still to be done — but he thinks of his time in Dorking as golden days with his growing family, with so many challenges in a changing world and with the success of the Anglican-Methodist venture as a particular source of quiet satisfaction. He and Marion are remembered with gratitude for all this by members of both congregations.

Chapter 7

Methodism in Dorking

"I preached at Dorking, and was much pleased with the congregation who seemed to taste the good word"

So wrote Revd. John Wesley in his Journal for 1 December 1774. In the previous year he had opened the Meeting House which continued in use for some 50 years until the Society which he had established in Dorking ceased to exist.

A revival began in 1834 and by 1850 the Society was strong enough to build a chapel in Back Lane (now Church Street). In 1901 a new and larger church was opened which was to dominate South Street for the next 73 years. In 1973 Methodists entered into an agreement to share premises with the Anglican church of St. Martin, the South Street premises were sold and the proceeds used to build what is now the Christian Centre.

This account describes some of the events which took place during the two and a quarter centuries following Wesley's first visit. It is a story of much devoted work by clergy and laymen many of whom can no longer be named; where names are mentioned they are the names of those who took part in some important event or names taken almost at random to add life to the narrative.

Details of the various buildings used for Methodist worship and a list of Methodist ministers who have been stationed in Dorking will be found at the end of this chapter. Methodist ministers are appointed to circuits comprising a number of Societies (i.e. churches) and not to particular places. When no minister was stationed there, the care of the Dorking Society would have been the responsibility of the circuit and when a minister was stationed in Dorking he likewise would have had responsibilities elsewhere.

John Wesley and Dorking

Wesley's first recorded visit to Dorking was on Thursday 12 January 1764. Next morning he preached "in a broad place not far from the Market-place". He was then 60 years old, but accustomed to riding prodigious distances on horseback and preaching to vast audiences in the open air. His first audience in Dorking however was two or three little children, but the numbers quickly increased "though the air was sharp and the ground exceeding wet". The next day he rode back to London, stopping to preach at Mitcham on the way. Later, when he took to travelling by chaise, he had a Dorking man as coachman.

Wesley did not visit Dorking again until 1770 when he began a series of more regular visits. By 1772 progress had been sufficient for the Society to acquire a Meeting House which Wesley himself opened. This building in Back Lane (Church Street) still stands behind no. 44 West Street and it is possible to discern the outline of the old windows in the brickwork on the east wall. Wesley took a continuing interest in the local Society; we know, for example, that in 1781 he made the journey to Dorking especially to conduct the burial of Mrs. Attersal "a lovely woman snatched away in the bloom of youth". On another visit he expressed himself as "much pleased with the congregation", but in 1790, not long before his death, he was moved to write:

"I went to Dorking, and laboured to awaken a harmless, honest, drowsy people, who for many years have seemed to stand stock still, neither increasing nor decreasing."

There are few records of Methodism in Dorking after Wesley's death. The local Society was probably still in existence in 1813 and the Meeting House was still being used for some years after that, but it was finally converted to other use and the local Society ceased to exist. Whether this was due to lack of leadership, controversy within the Society or, more likely, to increased competition from other churches in the town we do not know. Dorking was established as a stronghold of dissent long before John Wesley set foot there.

The Wesleyan Methodists come to Dorking

It was only after Wesley's death that Methodism became formally separated from the Church of England; in time, differences led to the establishment of separate bodies within Methodism the largest of which became the Wesleyan Methodist Church. Its critics would probably have said that this church had moved too far from Wesley's teaching and was assuming a mantle of bourgeois respectability! Certainly, its hierarchy gave scant support to the seven Methodist farm workers from Tolpuddle who were deported to Australia in 1834. By that time Dorking was developing into a thriving market town with a growing middle-class population. The main streets had been paved and lighting installed, there was a good number of shops, and residential villas and cottages were springing up around the town centre.

Not surprisingly, when Methodism returned to Dorking it was as part of the Wesleyan Methodist Church. About 1834 Samuel Beves, a watchmaker, moved to Dorking from Brighton and found no Methodists in the town. He slowly gathered a small group around him and after his marriage in 1836 preaching services began to be held on Sunday afternoons in the kitchen of his cottage in Heath Hill, Cotmandene. Some eight years later the Society comprised only seven full members. By then Dorking was under the care of the minister at Horsham some twelve miles away.

In 1842 the Horsham minister, Revd. Samuel Beard, began to make the journey to Dorking once a fortnight, preaching in the open air on alternate Tuesday evenings. Later that year he moved to Dorking, taking up residence in Rose Hill, and a room was rented for a meeting place. This room was on the south side of the High Street entered by a passage on the east of what is now Lloyds Bank; if not the same building it would have been near the present Salvation Army Hall. 1844 saw the establishment of the Dorking and Horsham Circuit with the Circuit Superintendent Minister resident in the town. Things were beginning to move, but even by 1845 total membership in the Circuit was only 95.

The First Church

The Society made good progress in the years that followed, probably helped by an influx of newcomers to the town, so that in less than ten years the meeting place on which much loving effort had been lavished was regarded as inconvenient. A plot of land was purchased, once again in Back Lane, and a "convenient, handy chapel" was built. It had 190 sittings, a stable and a burial ground, but neither school room nor vestry. Soon after it was opened in 1851 the Superintendent, Revd. John Owen, was able to report these attendance figures:

	Morning	Afternoon	Evening
General Congregation	56	36	107
Sunday Scholars	21	20	-

This chapel stood on the north side of what is now Church Street on a part of the site occupied today by Chapel Court. The foundation stones had been laid on 24 July 1850 by John Corderoy and Richard Gurney, two prominent Wesleyan laymen who had contributed generously to the building fund. John Corderoy, we know, was an influential member of the British and Foreign Schools Society, a non-denominational body which, because of opposition from some quarters, had become particularly involved in non-conformist education. The Dorking school, of which more anon, was on the opposite side of Back Lane to the chapel, so it is easy to see how John Corderoy's interest arose.

By 1856 Reigate and Redhill had been added to the circuit and in the following year Leatherhead, but by 1866 the circuit membership was only 146 leaving it numerically still one of the smallest circuits in the whole of British Methodism. In that year the Superintendent Minister's residence was moved to Redhill and from then until 1897 there was no minister living in Dorking.

It is clear from the figures already quoted that the congregations in Dorking far exceeded the numbers who were prepared to commit themselves to membership. The chapel was enlarged in 1883, the new building having seating for an additional 160 people with rooms underneath for the very popular Sunday School. A Dorking guide of 1888 described it as "a substantial and neat building of red-brick, with stone front ornamented by a circular doorway, and two corner towers. Over the entrance is a large window and the structure is altogether well lit".

A Victorian Minister

Revd. John Nelson is perhaps typical of the 13 Wesleyan Ministers who worked in Dorking at the middle of the century, each moving on after one or two years as was then customary. He was a Yorkshireman, born in Bradford and 36 years old when, with his family, he moved to Dorking in 1856. His house in Arundel Road he himself described as not having "dimensions commensurate with the requirements of a large family". Characteristically it was the comfort of his successor not his own comfort that gave him concern. Working from this house he was for two years from September 1856 in sole charge of a circuit which stretched some 20 miles from north to south and 15 miles from east to west. Although the Reading Guildford and Reigate Railway had been opened in 1849 there was as yet no railway running north-south through Dorking. Perhaps like Wesley he rode to his appointments on horseback — we do not know.

It was said that he thought much of the deep things of God and that "to his intelligent listeners his sermons were full of suggestions and rich in comfort". However he was no

The first Methodist Meeting Place, Back Lane, a watercolour of c1800.

Edith Corderoy (1841-1938).

Charles Degenhardt (1876-1956) in his garden with two great nieces.

intellectual sluggard, for each quarter he preached between 60 and 70 times, visiting each of the 13 preaching places in the circuit at least once and administering the sacrament at each of the principal places. Horsham, for example, he visited regularly once a month, preaching there on Sunday morning and evening with an afternoon service at Mannings Heath. Redhill he visited twice a quarter, again preaching twice on Sunday with an afternoon service at Reigate. Then he preached every other Monday evening at Reigate and every other Wednesday evening at Effingham. So it went on, with four or five Sundays at Dorking to be worked into his programme.

A farmer's wife said that he looked on his circuit as a farm and expected a return from every field! After leaving Dorking he was to continue in the active ministry for another 31 years before retiring, still active, to New Zealand where he died in 1902.

Some Victorian Laymen

Methodist property has traditionally been owned and looked after by Trustees. By the middle of the century Dorking had about 3500 inhabitants with almost as many again living in the busy agricultural communities which surrounded it so it is not surprising that many of the first Trustees of the new Chapel were farmers and tradesmen. To name a few: John Coulson, farmer; John Stringer, upholsterer; James Well, grocer; Charles Chitty, cordwainer; Amos Loxley, farmer; Henry Cole, carrier.

The last named Henry Cole had come to Dorking in 1842 as a young man of 22 and lived to see the new church opened in South Street. He was to become an important businessman and Cole's Leather shop in Dorking High Street which he opened in 1842 did not close until 1974. He owned a tannery, his son Alfred had a builder's business in West Street and there were leather shops in Guildford, Brighton and London. In his old age he was described as "the Father of Dorking Methodism". He was certainly one of its fathers for he began preaching when he arrived in Dorking and is credited with prodigious walks to take his preaching appointments. In 1844, for example, he was preaching on five Sundays a quarter and in the summer of 1857 on almost every Sunday, taking in his stride appointments at Ockley, Oakwood Hill, Westhumble and Leatherhead — many of the services being on Sunday evenings and not starting until 6.30 (no daylight saving then!).

Henry Cole was by no means the only active local preacher in the middle of the century. John Coulson, a farmer from Great Bookham, was preaching no fewer than 25 times in one quarter to places as far distant as Horsham, Redhill and Effingham — perhaps he too travelled on horseback! Samuel Beves was still active and preaching as far away as Ockley, Leatherhead and Reigate. Then, as the century drew to its close, more Wesleyan families moved into the town.

In 1883, there came to Dorking F.W. Doubleday who was to be a leading citizen as well as a leader in the church. His chemist's shop and dentistry (now Woodcocks) occupied a prominent position by the White Horse in the High Street. Like other businessmen of his day he lived over his shop until he moved to Wyngate House in South Street (now Waitrose) to concentrate on his dentist's practice there. With his wife's family the Nicklins, he threw himself into the work of the church and circuit. He was to be a Circuit Steward in the important years at the turn of the century when the new church was being built and a Trustee of the new church for no fewer than 27 years. Rosa, the eldest of their five children, was to be an active Methodist almost until her death in 1973 and their two sons, Fred (later Revd. F.N. Doubleday) and Hugh, were to become well-known at St. Martin's parish church.

And the Ladies

As it was not customary for ladies to hold office and it would have been outside the law for a lady to act as Trustee, we know less about them than we do about the men. They certainly played an important part in the Victorian church and were indispensable to the running of the large and flourishing Sunday School which was central to its work.

One happy outcome of the connection with the Corderoy family was the interest of John Corderoy's niece Edith who moved to Dorking in 1880, first occupying a house in Cliftonville and then building her own home on the new Holloway Farm Estate at Knoll Road. She was to be an indefatigable worker for the church for over 50 years. Writing in 1894 she said "I hate bazaars and such", but then proceeded to unveil her plans for just such an event! Although she added "We work slowly at Dorking" the ladies there must have had much to occupy their time. She became well known in the town through her work as treasurer of the Dorking British School when it became clear in 1894 that the school's premises in Back Lane were likely to be condemned. It is a matter of history that it was only as a result of her determined efforts, combined with the generosity of Mr. T.E. Powell of St. Martin's, that the school that now bears their joint names was saved.

On 15 January 1894 an event occurred at the Circuit Quarterly Meeting which was to have far-reaching consequences. Miss Catherina Dawson of Redhill was appointed Circuit Steward to serve with Mr. F.W. Doubleday of Dorking. The appointment of a lady was unusual but was universally welcomed in the circuit. She became a representative to the District Synod where she was again welcomed and from there she was elected a representative to the Wesleyan Methodist Conference. At this point she became a national figure. Laymen had only been admitted to the Conference in 1878 and a strong body of clergy would have barred her entry on the grounds that a woman could not be a layman! In the event she was allowed to attend Conference where she behaved impeccably and the matter was solved by referring it to a committee. A year later the committee, thinking amongst other things that it was not probable that many women would wish to be elected, recommended the admission of women representatives. Alas for women's rights, the Conference of 1895 thought it knew better and rejected the recommendation.

The New Church in South Street

As the 19th century drew to its close the 1842 chapel began to seem inadequate. Church Street, as it was called by then, was not the fashionable quarter that it is today, the premises were not large enough for the Sunday School now grown to 130 children and the leaders looked for a site more worthy, as they saw it, of the growing status of Methodism in the town. This view was shared by the Superintendent Minister at Redhill. Under his direction, two young probationer ministers did good work in the town and then in 1897 a minister was once more stationed in Dorking, a Building Committee was established and in 1899 a new site was purchased in South Street. Some local people were not too pleased at the demolition of a shop and cottages on the site, but building commenced and on 26 January 1901 the new church was opened.

The church itself stood on the south corner of Vincent Road on land running almost 200 feet down that road. The frontage on South Street was built in the Gothic style looking very much a church with its 90 foot spire, but inside it was a traditional non-conformist plan with seating in the church and gallery for 470 people. Next to the church a separate building, known as Wesley Hall, also facing South Street, was built in the same style as the church. A vestry and church rooms at the back joined the two buildings and with the hall provided excellent premises for Sunday School work and church gatherings. Finally, in 1905 a new organ was installed in the church and that same year the buildings were wired for electricity. The church leaders would rightly have felt that they had achieved their objective of building a worthy place of worship.

These buildings were to serve the needs of Methodism in Dorking for the next 73 years. Over this long period many alterations were carried out and changes made to modernise the interiors. In the church the entrance vestibule was enlarged, the number of sittings was reduced, the text over the pulpit was replaced by a cross and amplifying equipment was installed, while alterations to the church rooms included the creation of a new kitchen and Sunday School rooms. Nevertheless, as time went by the condition of the fabric began to give the Trustees increasing concern. A new slate-tiled roof was fixed in 1964 and other major repairs were then becoming necessary.

Progress at South Street

In 1902 Dorking again became the head of a Dorking and Horsham Circuit with much the same boundaries as it has today, sensibly following the line of the railway which by then ran from Leatherhead through Dorking to Horsham and beyond. Travel would not have been the difficult undertaking that it had been and, later, the advent of the motor car, although an expensive luxury for Methodist ministers, made it even easier. A garage was erected at the Methodist manse in Westcott Road in 1929, but as late as 1960 the Superintendent, Revd. James Isherwood, was still travelling his circuit in all weathers on an early moped.

As first Superintendent of the new circuit, Revd. John Telford moved to Dorking in 1902. He was already well known in Methodism as a historian and administrator and when Superintendent of the Redhill circuit he had been the guiding hand behind the building of the new Dorking church. The Society was to owe much to his experience and leadership in its early days at South Street. In 1905 he moved to an appointment in London but continued to live in Dorking, where he was well known, until his death in 1936.

At first, the church and Sunday School both thrived in the new premises. The number of full members increased from 76 in 1902 to 117 in 1909 but there or thereabouts it has remained to this day. It is hard to explain this disappointing lack of growth at a time when Dorking itself has been expanding rapidly. The Great War of 1914-18 in which no fewer than 15 young men from the church lost their lives was certainly one factor, the loss of some families by removal and others by death was another, but these things affected other more successful churches elsewhere. Commitment and enthusiasm have had to make up for lack of numbers; the Society has continued to witness in the town and has been strong enough to make its mark on the life of Dorking.

Some People at South Street Church

The church leaders at the beginning of the 20th century were local businessmen and tradesmen. Charles Degenhardt, whose home and drapery shop (now the Abbey National and an adjoining shop) stood on the north side of South Street not far from Pump Corner, was Trust Secretary from 1910 to 1943 and Trust Treasurer from 1913 to 1947. Old members have affectionate memories of him tending his garden which was behind the shops on the other side of the High Street, or perhaps sitting there reading his Shakespeare. William Poole, a local preacher, did not approve of Sunday travel by rail. In his old age he recalled that, having shut up his draper's shop in the High Street late on Saturday night, he had to rise early the next morning to walk the 12 miles to Horsham if he was required to take a service there. He was said to be the first person in Dorking to own a wireless set. Later Will Robins, whose family business still continues at 224 High Street, was choirmaster from 1921 to 1947. He had been 30 years ahead of his time in 1924 when the Trustees found that 'the time was not ripe' to adopt his suggestion that the Lord's prayer might be sung and not said.

Significantly, Charles Degenhardt's successor as Trust Secretary was not a local businessman. Jack Blake, who held this post from 1947 until he left Dorking in 1963, was a distinguished civil servant who was later to be Vice-President of the Methodist Conference. He was also one of many talented organists, male and female, who served the South Street church. This organ was an excellent one which was passed on to another Methodist church when the buildings were demolished and was often in use for pleasure and practice. At first it had been blown by hand and it is amusing to find that when an electric motor was installed in 1905 the Trustees were so concerned at the cost of electricity that they considered disconnecting the motor on weekdays. In the end they fixed a tariff of 4d. an hour for church members and 6d. for others.

In the 1960s a group of young people led by a local policeman, Bert Kingswood, were allowed to clear the rubble under the hall, where there had been a public air-raid shelter, and to build rooms for a club. With the blessing of the church they established there "The Cellar Club" which did great work as a meeting place for young people from the town and district right up to the end of 1973 when the premises were sold.

Ladies continued to play an important role in the church and Sunday School and over the years there were several lady organists. Later, they also began to figure amongst the church officers, Joan Stampe, the first lady Local Preacher, being appointed in 1948 and Jean Pullinger, the first lady Church Steward, in 1971. When a new Trust was formed in 1972, seven of the 23 Trustees were ladies included for the first time.

The Ecumenical Movement

The new building in South Street was sometimes referred to as a church and sometimes as a chapel but there is little doubt that at the beginning of the century the religious and

Methodist Church, South Street, a drawing by Geoffrey Fletcher of 1959.

The Revd. Ronald Rawlings with the Revd. Jack Roundhill in St. Martin's churchyard, photograph taken in 1973.

social distinction between "Church" and "Chapel" was as marked in Dorking as elsewhere in the country. Although the vicar of St. Martin's was a respected figure in the town the relations between the two congregations were certainly not as harmonious as they are today! These are some of the replies that Edith Corderoy received to invitations to a public meeting held in 1895 about the plight of the Dorking British School:

> "I have not the least desire to interfere in any way with any of my neighbours in their efforts to keep up an undenominational school"   Lord Ashcombe

> "I am one of those who wish to live and let live. However much I must differ with others it is not for me to hinder their good works, and any attempt at religious bigotry or intolerance will not meet with my approval or consent"
> The Vicar of St. Martin's

The vicar of St. Paul's was unable to be present but wished the meeting every success. In 1912, as we have seen, Neville Stiff could see the good work being done by other denominations and look forward to the reunion of Christendom.

On 20 September 1932 the Methodist Church did something to put its house in order when the provisions of the Methodist Church Act, 1929, came into force providing for the union of the Wesleyan Methodist Church with the Primitive Methodist Church and the United Methodist Church. Although a national event not affecting Dorking directly, this must have had its local significance and was surely an indication of changing attitudes.

In March 1943 the Anglican parishes of St. Martin and St. Paul came together with the Congregational, Baptist and Methodist churches to establish the "Dorking Council of Churches for Religion and Life" soon to incorporate the "Dorking Christian Youth Group" and to be re-named the "Dorking Council of Churches". Methodists enthusiastically supported this venture, providing lay officers from the outset, and the Council was able to promote joint services, lectures and events in the town as well as to provide a forum for inter-church co-operation. From this beginning has evolved the close relations between the churches in the town and the much more widely based Council that exists today.

Towards Church Unity

In the years following the Second World War hope for church union ran high. Conversations took place at national level and some successes were achieved, so when Revd. Ronald Rawlings came to Dorking in 1967 the subject was very much in the air. His experience as secretary of the District Synod was to prove invaluable in leading the Dorking Society through a maze of discussions and negotiations with other churches in the town.

In 1969 the Dorking Congregational Church Meeting invited Baptists and Methodists to meet with them to discuss the possibilities of joint work and witness. Meetings between the three local churches followed and in October 1969 the Congregational and Methodist churches committed themselves to exploring, during the following twelve months, the possibility of forming a United Church. During that year joint services were held on an experimental basis, church members met together and a Joint Commission was established which prepared a draft constitution for a United Church. In the event, the Commission's scheme did not prove acceptable and the proposals had to be laid aside.

At that very time, Revd. Jack Roundhill, vicar of St. Martin's, approached the Methodists with a most generous and welcome invitation from his church. Recent legislation had made it possible to allow the use of Anglican premises by other churches and the invitation was to consider entering into an agreement for shared use of St. Martin's. The offer was accepted. Most harmonious discussions took place, Methodists were allowed to hold experimental services in St. Martin's, working parties were established and church members consulted. The far-reaching plan that emerged is reflected in the arrangements in force today. Anglicans agreed to grant equal rights to the use of the parish church and to sell the church halls and verger's cottage to the Methodists at a very reasonable price. Methodists in return agreed to sell their premises in South Street, to use the proceeds to reconstruct the halls and to grant equal use of the new premises (The Christian Centre) to Anglicans. Methodists began to use St. Martin's for regular worship on 7 January 1973, a Sharing Agreement for the church was signed on 17 June 1973, the Methodist premises in South Street were sold on 18 January 1974 and the agreement for the halls was signed on 7 March 1976. Finally, with Anglican support and after much hard work to the building, the Cellar Club, appropriately re-named 'The Crypt Club', moved into a new club room under St. Martin's church. (*See* also Chapter 6).

St. Martin's Methodist Church

So the church has been called since its move.

Revd. Ronald Rawlings remained at Dorking to lead the Society through almost three years of regular worship at St. Martin's and to see the plans for the Christian Centre near completion. It fell to his successors, Revd. Bill Murphy and Revd. John Hope, to build on his work. Bill Murphy in particular not only had to absorb a new situation, but also to oversee the completion of the Christian Centre, to make arrangements with the Dorking Council of Churches for its management and to develop working relations with Anglicans. The present happy state owes much to the enthusiasm, hard work and personalities of these three ministers.

Some future historian will be better able to assess this great adventure, involving as it did the forsaking of time-honoured buildings for worship in very different surroundings, but Methodists can look back on the last 17 years with some satisfaction. Not everyone had been able to accept the move, some because they could not come to terms with the demolition of the old church and some because, as they saw it, Methodist worship would lose something vital in the unfamiliar surroundings of a parish church. This latter factor has perhaps also influenced some Methodists who have since moved into Dorking and chosen to worship elsewhere, although, interestingly, some of those who left the church in 1973 rejoined later. The greater numbers worshipping in the Shared Church give better opportunities, particularly for young people, than there had been in the later years at South Street and despite its initial membership losses the Methodist Society seems as strong in 1990 as it was 17 years ago. The Christian Centre, now run by a committee drawn from the churches of Dorking, has certainly been a success story; it is well used and is a base for real christian outreach.

"The People Called Methodists"

We know all too little about what went on inside the church over the years described in this history. From the earliest days the Wesleys had instituted a system of classes, the members of each Society "being divided into smaller companies, called classes, according to their respective places of abode" and each class having an appointed leader who was expected to meet the ministers and stewards weekly to inform them of the state of his class. Class meetings for prayer and fellowship were held weekly and attendance was an obligation of membership. Such meetings would have been a central feature probably until well into the present century, but increasing pressures of life, amongst other things, have gradually brought regular meetings to an end. However, the organisation into classes continues as an essential link between members and their minister while the intimacy of the class has to some extent been replaced by House Groups.

Methodists always had available a book of services based on the Book of Common Prayer, which would have been followed in the administration of the sacraments and for other special occasions, but it seems unlikely that the order for morning prayer was used in the Victorian church. If it was, the custom must have been discontinued because, in this century, it was not until the fifties that the Leaders' Meeting approved its occasional use. Hymn singing must always have been an important feature and free prayer and, above all, preaching have surely been the norm throughout most of the years described.

We hope that strangers have always been made welcome; as recently as 1949 the church was commended for its enlightened attitude in inviting hikers to attend evening service "in hiking kit"! The social conscience inspired by Wesley himself has always been important and the strict standards set by our Methodist fathers would have been one feature to set them apart from the Established Church. Support for missionary activities, too, has a long history in Dorking. We know of successful meetings for foreign mission being organised as early as 1842; after the 1843 meeting, held on Boxing Day, it was noted that "the evening was unfavourable but the proceeds were more than double those of last year". The Sunday School was always regarded as most important and there is a history of campaigns to seek out new scholars right to the present day.

In the less sophisticated days before the media had invaded our homes the church was a centre also for social activities and fellowship. This must have been so in the last century as we know it has been in this. Within living memory drama evenings, a sports club, meetings of the Wesley Guild and a Young Wives Group as well as of Guides and Brownies were regular events. The Women's Fellowship which celebrated its 50th Anniversary in 1989 was the successor to a Woman's Social Hour. This apart, few of these activities survive today.

As Dorking has evolved, so in the church local businessmen, tradesmen and farmers no longer predominate; families do not stay in the town for generations; many members now are professional men and women and business people who find Dorking a pleasant place in which to have their homes while earning their livings elsewhere; among the older members too are some who have only come to Dorking on retirement. Pensioners some of us may be, but there is an encouraging number of younger families and a thriving "Seekers Finders" Sunday School.

L'Envoi

Although the Sharing Agreements were nothing more than undertakings to allow each church to use the other's premises on agreed terms, something more was hoped for and planned for from the beginning. The close working that has been achieved between the two churches is something for which we can certainly give thanks. The clergy can be seen to be working together, the PCC and the Methodist Church Council meet together doing their business as one body, joint committees have long been established and joint meetings, conferences and other events are the accepted norm. Joint Confirmation Services are held at which all those newly confirmed are accepted into membership of both churches. There is a jointly appointed organist and choirmaster. Although the two churches continue to hold their separate services on most Sunday mornings, the two congregations worship together at all the great Christian festivals and on many other occasions in the year.

It is not easy to see how we are called to make further progress in Dorking until the two mother churches come to some accord. Historical reasons make it understandable that not all members of the two congregations regard their coming together with equal enthusiasm, but we surely have a God-given opportunity, not yet open to many church people, to explore our relationship at deeper levels whilst yet retaining separate identities. Methodism has gained much but would have much to contribute to a closer union. It can provide a special link with other non-conformist churches in the town, it seems to have a good system of administration and decision-making and, in the writer's view, has much to offer in worship and outlook.

Appendix A
Methodist Places of Worship in Dorking

Meeting House in Back Lane (now Church Street)
Opened on 27 November 1772 by Revd. John Wesley.
Probably ceased to be used sometime after 1813.

Meeting Place off the High Street
A rented building situated on the south side of the High Street entered by a passage "on the east of the London and County Bank".
Registered as a Place of Public Worship on 26 August 1842.
Ceased to be used in 1851.

Church in Back Lane (now Church Street)
Foundation stones laid on 24 July 1850 by Mr. John Corderoy and Mr. Thomas Gurney. Cost: land £200, building £850. Opened 1851. Registered as a place of Public Worship on 29 September 1854.
To mark the enlargement of the church, stones were laid on 28 June 1883 by:
    Miss Edith Corderoy, of Dorking, who re-laid the stone laid by her uncle John Corderoy

Miss Mary Cole, of Dorking, on behalf of teachers and scholars
Mrs Duncan, Miss Dawson and Miss Hedley of Redhill
Mrs Chard of Highgate
The enlargement cost £1,400.
Ceased to be used 1901. Sold for £800.

Church in South Street
Situated on the south corner of Vincent Road, with frontage on South Street and access from Vincent Road at the rear.
Architect: Frederick Boreham, F.R.I.B.A. of London
Foundation stones laid on 23 May 1900:

Wesley Hall	By Mr. T.C. Warner
	Mr. & Mrs. G.T. Nicklin
	Revd. A.D. Smart
	Mr. James Woodley
	Mr. R.W. Wiles
The Church	By Mrs. R. Harker (The Bletchingley Stone)
	Mrs. C.H. Ward (The Reigate Stone)
	Mrs Telford*
	Major Hart of Stanford
	Miss Wesley Marshall on behalf of Miss Wyburn
	Mrs. Horace B. Marshall of Streatham*
	Mr. & Mrs. Doubleday*
	Mr. W.C. Nicklin*
	Mr. & Mrs. Mont Smith

Wesley Hall was opened on 14 November 1900 by Mr. Henry Cole.
The church was opened on 24 January 1901 by Miss Edith Corderoy.
Cost: land £1,400, building £6,000, organ £400.
Re-opened after alterations on 23 January 1960 by Miss Rosa Doubleday.
Sold January 1974 for £226,000.

The Christian Centre
Built from St. Martin's church rooms and verger's cottage on the west side of St. Martin's churchyard.
Architect: Robert Potter, F.R.I.B.A., F.S.A. of Brandt, Potter and Partners, Southampton.
Opened on 18 September 1977 by Brian Worth, Treasurer, the British Council of Churches.
The four stones from the South Street church marked * were re-laid in the Centre.
Cost: purchase of site £19,500, building £183,500. The balance of the sale proceeds, after purchase of the new manse in Sondes Place Drive, were transferred to the Circuit Development Fund.
Under the Sharing Agreement dated 7 March 1976 Methodists and Anglicans have equal rights to the use of the Centre and equal responsibility for maintenance.

N.B. Under an Agreement dated 17 June 1973 both churches had equal rights to the use of the parish church with Methodists responsible for only 10% (since increased) of maintenance costs.

Appendix B
Methodist Ministers Stationed in Dorking

Appointments are for twelve months from September in each of the years stated.

1842	Samuel Beard
1843	William Wilson
1844-45	Aaron Langley
1846	William Way
1847	George Clement
1848-50	John Owen
1851	Edward Crofts
1852-54	Alexander Puddicombe
1855	William Badeley
1856-57	John Nelson
1858-60	Henry J. Thomas
1861-63	William Jackson
1864-65	John Bate

From September 1866 to August 1897 there was no minister stationed in Dorking, the Superintendent Minister being resident in Redhill. Prior to the appointment of a minister in 1897, the Superintendent was assisted by two young ministers George R. Forde and Charles C. Scraggs, who worked in Dorking.

1897-98	Edward Grainger
1899-01	Arthur D. Smart
1902-4	John Telford
1905	John H. Lockley
1906-8	Joseph H. Hopkins
1909-11	Jabez Ingram
1912-14	Richard E. Brown
1915-18	Frederick J. Harvey
1919-20	Henry W. Shrewsbury
1921-25	Walter Norton
1926-28	T. Leonard Climer
1929-33	John W. Stanlake
1934-37	Ernest J. Jones
1938-39	Arthur W. Sheldon

1940-43	E. Evans
1944-48	Eric G. Frost
1949-53	Geoffrey H. Crosby
1954-56	Ernest H. Lawrence
1957-60	James Isherwood
1961-66	John W. Watson
1967-74	Ronald S. Rawlings
1975-83	William (Bill) Murphy
1984-	John L. Hope

Chapter 8

St. Barnabas Church, Ranmore

St. Barnabas church, Ranmore, was built in 1859 at the sole expense of Mr. George Cubitt, (1828-1917). An estate church, it was intended to serve the growing number of people employed on the Cubitt family's recently acquired estate of Denbies on the outskirts of Dorking. George Cubitt was a man who had close connections with the church in Dorking, for his wife Laura, whom he had married in 1853, was the daughter of the Revd. James Joyce and the sister of the Revd. William H. Joyce, both of whom were vicars of St. Martin's. He had inherited the Denbies estate on Ranmore Common from his father, Thomas, in 1855.

The Cubitt Family and the Denbies Estate

Thomas Cubitt had become a millionaire by revolutionising the building trades in London. He was the first man to purchase land and build complete houses for sale, and was responsible for developing much of Bloomsbury and Belgravia. In so doing he established such a good reputation that he was commissioned by Queen Victoria to build Osborne House on the Isle of Wight between 1845 and 1851. He purchased Denbies in 1850 from Lord Londesborough. The estate consisted of over 3,900 acres covering much of the northern part of Dorking down to the Pippbrook, including what is now the Meadowbank recreation ground, Parkway and Fairfield Drive, as well as a large area to the west of the town, including Sondes Farm, which had been purchased early in the 19th century by William Denison, Lord Londesborough's grandfather. Denbies House was an old Georgian mansion built around 1760 by Jonathan Tyers, owner of the Vauxhall Pleasure Gardens, and it did not meet Thomas Cubitt's exacting requirements. He immediately set about replacing it with a new mansion in an Italianate style similar to that of the east wing of Osborne House. It is said that he was aiming to rival Deepdene House which stood on the south side of Dorking. The house had only just been completed when he died on 20 December 1855.

Like many wealthy philanthropists of the mid-19th century, both Thomas Cubitt and his son George were concerned about the plight of the working classes in an increasingly industrialised and urban society. Throughout his life Thomas campaigned against increasing air pollution and for improvements in sewage disposal and George, as Member of Parliament for Mid-Surrey from 1860, also took an active part in trying to improve social conditions. It was an age when many felt that the only answer to the social ills of Victorian England was a return to the countryside and the establishment of new rural communities, and undoubtedly Thomas and George Cubitt saw the acquisition of Denbies as an opportunity to establish such a community on Ranmore for those employed at the house and on the adjacent farms. It was with this in mind that George Cubitt built not only the church and rectory, but also a school for the children on the estate. In addition, further along the common, he built the Dispensary, which not only provided treatment for the sick, but was also a training establishment for single girls from the estate wishing to go into service both at Denbies House and elsewhere. It was his intention to provide for both the physical and the spiritual welfare of his employees. His interest in this field led to his being appointed Church Estates Commissioner in 1874. In 1880 he became a member of the Privy Council and in 1892 he was elevated to the peerage as Baron Ashcombe of Dorking and Bodiam Castle.

The Church

St. Barnabas church was designed by Sir George Gilbert Scott (1811-1878), the architect who is famous not only for the restoration of many of England's cathedrals, but also for the building of the Albert Memorial and St. Pancras Station in London. He was a very busy architect who worked with a large office and sometimes his buildings could be dull and repetitive. The church of St. Barnabas, however, benefits from its site on the ridge of the North Downs and from having had plenty of money available for its construction. It is a particularly good and original example of his work in the Gothic Revival style. The design of the exterior of the church is deceptively simple but strong: faced in flint with bands and quoins of Bath stone, it is dominated by a central octagonal tower and spire which soars to a height of nearly 150 ft, 700 ft above sea level. Visible for miles around — they say that on a clear day you can see it from the Crystal Palace — the spire was a source of amusement amongst Cubitt's friends, including the author George Meredith, who lived locally. They suggested it represented his finger pointing up to heaven!

The comparative austerity of the exterior of the church provides little clue to the lavish design of the interior which makes extensive use of marble and elaborate carving. It has survived almost unaltered, with all its original fittings, including many of the original rush kneelers in the splendid oak pews. The plan is cruciform with nave and chancel separated by the central tower, and north and south transepts, the north now containing the organ, the south the Cubitt chapel. Undoubtedly the most striking feature is the reredos of cream alabaster behind the altar which occupies the full width of the chancel. It is richly ornamented with diaperwork and carved foliage picked out in gold, and in the arcading on either side are carved the Apostles' Creed, the Lord's Prayer and the Ten Commandments. The altar itself is not original, but was donated to the church in 1905 in memory of Laura, Lady Ashcombe, by her surviving children, together with the marble pavement on which it stands. It contrasts strikingly with the only memorial in the church to its founder, a simple bronze plaque on the wall to the south of the altar which depicts George Cubitt dressed in his peer's robes, kneeling and offering the church up to God.

The east window was a gift from the Revd. Charles and Mrs. Parker, with stained glass by J.G. Crace, who was principally an interior decorator but who had also worked with A.W.N. Pugin, the great gothic revivalist, between 1842 and Pugin's death in 1852. It depicts scenes taken from the life of Christ: the Annunciation, the Nativity, the Crucifixion, the Entombment and the Resurrection, with, in the quatrefoil window above, Christ in Majesty. The rest of the stained glass in the church was by Clayton and Bell.

In the chancel the jambs of the deeply recessed windows are enriched with clusters of shafts in Devonshire red marble, whilst beneath the tower the four massive arches of the crossing are supported by similar clusters in a variety of marbles and polished stone. Each shaft is decorated with a carved stone capital of naturalistic foliage. The disproportionately large size of the capitals on the piers in the crossing has led to the suggestion that Scott originally intended to use them elsewhere in a larger building but this is most improbable in such a carefully designed church. The pulpit, which stands on a marble and granite plinth, is faced in red Mansfield stone, and decorated with medallions of the four evangelists set in alabaster quatrefoils; the bookrest, an integral part of the design, is supported by a marble shaft. Similarly, the font at the back of the church also stands on a granite plinth, and is constructed in black and maroon marble with an elaborate bronze lid. All the details are rich, but in sombre colours, giving a strong and dramatic effect.

Work on the building of the church began in June 1858. The original site chosen was slightly further to the west of the existing church but it proved impossible to secure a firm foundation. It was therefore decided to move the whole project eastward, closer to the school which was then nearing completion. The foundation stone was eventually laid on 18 September 1858, four months later than intended, and the building work was completed a year later. The consecration of the church, dedicated to St. Barnabas, by the Bishop of Winchester took place on All Saints' Day, 1 November 1859, and the anniversary was celebrated each year until the First World War with a special morning service to which a guest preacher was invited. The parish of Ranmore was not created until 1860. Made up of parts of the parishes of Dorking, Mickleham, Effingham and Great and Little Bookham it covers an area of 2,000 acres, roughly half the size of the Denbies estate as it then was.

The Early Life of the Church

The church's close involvement with the life of Denbies ensured that until the outbreak of the Second World War in 1939 it thrived. Over 300 people were employed on the estate and all were expected to attend church regularly. The indoor servants at the house were given an hour off on Sundays specifically to attend one of the three church services held each Sunday: Holy Communion at 8.00 a.m., mattins at 11.00 a.m. and evensong at 6.00 p.m. Each person had his or her allotted place in the pews, the Cubitt family always sitting at the front on the right hand side (a tradition which persists to this day). Additional services were held on weekdays attended by the children from the school, who were also given daily scripture lessons by the rector. Interestingly, the records show that although the church was usually full because people were expected to attend, the number of communicants was not large, and only a small percentage were in fact confirmed as members of the church. Employees on the estate were not only expected to attend church, they were also expected to make an active contribution to its life. The flowers on the main altar, for instance, were for many years arranged by Lady Ashcombe's secretary. Others were involved as bellringers, sidesmen, cleaners, members of the choir, organ blowers, and in many other ways, for the church and the school were the focus of the community. The Cubitt family always remained in firm control of church affairs, however, for successive members of the family acted as rector's warden and the clergy themselves were appointed by Lord Ashcombe as patron of the living.

St. Barnabas Church, Ranmore.

North-west view.

Interior view looking east, an engraving of c1860.

The Cubitts of Denbies.

Memorial plaque to George, first Baron Ashcombe (1828-1917), on the south wall of the chancel.

Henry Archibald Cubitt (1892-1916), an oil painting by Lance Calkin, 1918.

Henry, second Baron Ashcombe (1867-1947), Lord Lieutenant of Surrey 1905-39, an oil painting by Sir William Llewellyn, 1931.

118

The Cubitt chapel, St. Barnabas Church, Ranmore, the altarpiece and mural paintings by E. Reginald Frampton, 1918-19.

The Rector of Ranmore, the Revd. Martyn Farrant, at the service of Holy Communion on 21 January 1990.

Charities

The church on Ranmore provided for the welfare of its parishioners through its Sick and Poor Fund. Money was raised for the fund through offertory collections, as were the church's regular donations to the Dorking Moral Welfare Society. Each year the Sick and Poor Fund made a donation to the church's Clothing Club, whose members themselves made a weekly contribution. The money was used to provide adequate clothing for the members. The church accounts for 1912/13 show deposits from members of £50.17s.10d. and a donation from the church of £7.2s.0d. This, together with a further donation of £5.0s.0d., probably from Lord Ashcombe himself, was used to purchase goods from local suppliers, including Degenhardts, whose shop in South Street only closed in the late 1970s. The accounts show that the club had 37 members in that year, each of whom received a cash payment of 6d. in addition to the clothes provided. After the First World War the Clothing Club was administered by the PCC, whose first meeting was held in the schoolroom on Saturday 10 April, 1920. It was the PCC who in 1932 renamed it the Ranmore Thrift Club and agreed that in future the money should be spent on 'necessaries'.

Social Events

Also in 1932 it was proposed by the PCC that the church should form a tennis club, and three years later, with the help of a generous donation of £120 from Lord Ashcombe, a court was laid out on a piece of land adjacent to the Dispensary, complete with a small pavilion. Virtually all the indoor staff from Denbies became members and a tennis tournament was held each year until the outbreak of the Second World War. The winners of the singles tournaments each won a silver cup, and there were other prizes to the value of 5/-. The committee was chaired by the rector, and, as well as the tournaments, organised dances and beetle drives in the school hall and an annual summer outing. The church thus also became a focus of the community's social life. The success of the tennis club, however, caused a marked reduction in attendance at church during the summer months, and in 1942 it was decided that the court should be closed during the hours of the church services! By then the annual tournaments had had to be suspended because so many members had been called up into the armed forces, and after the war there was insufficient support for them to be revived. In 1950 it was decided to let the court out on an hourly basis and a few years later the club was wound up.

The Cubitt Chapel

In the First World War, Henry, second Baron Ashcombe, (1867-1947) lost his three eldest sons, all of whom were in their twenties. Henry Archibald Cubitt, the heir to the barony was killed on 15 September 1916 whilst serving as a captain in the Coldstream Guards. In the following year a faculty was sought by his family to convert the south transept of the church into a chapel in his memory. By the time that permission had been obtained his brother Alick George had also been killed in action whilst serving as a Lieutenant in the XVth Hussars and William Hugh had died of wounds sustained as a Lieutenant in the 1st Royal Dragoons.

The Cubitt chapel, as it is now known, was dedicated by the Bishop of Winchester in

June 1919. It is separated from the main body of the church by an oak parclose screen. The altar and pavement in memory of Henry Archibald are in Greek marble and there are tablets on either side of the altar in memory of his two brothers. The altarpiece shows the Adoration of the Magi and is surrounded by a carved stone frieze of angels holding symbols of the Passion. The mural paintings on the wall above, like the altarpiece, are by E. Reginald Frampton (1872-1923). The son of a stained-glass artist, Frampton was a most interesting painter, who was particularly influenced by Puvis de Chavannes and Burne-Jones. He executed several important mural commissions early in his career before he turned to teaching. The subjects of his pictures were frequently religious scenes or landscapes. The murals here seem to be an isolated example at this period of his life before his early death. The technique used is known as spirit fresco, the altarpiece on a specially prepared absorbent ground and the murals directly onto the stone. The iconography is complex and is centred around the Adoration of the Magi. Above the altarpiece are three figures hovering over a rainbow, the central one holding the star of Bethlehem. They are placed between the virtues of Faith, Hope and Charity on one side, and Peace, Justice and Fortitude on the other. Below them the patron saints of England, France and Belgium, with other figures gathered around a kneeling knight, all worship the Christ Child. The frescoes are in muted pastel shades.

In 1981 a tablet in green Westmorland slate was donated by the respective families of the second Baron's three remaining sons, who had survived the Great War. It commemorates Roland Calvert Cubitt, third Baron Ashcombe (1899-1962), Archibald Edward Cubitt (1901-1972) and Charles Guy Cubitt (1903-1979).

The Decline of the Estate and the Church

11 other members of the Ranmore parish were also killed in the First World War. A plaque in their memory, on the south wall of the nave, was dedicated by the Bishop of Winchester at a special service on 11 June 1922 (St. Barnabas Day). Beneath it is a plaque to Edward George Baker. He was the only parishioner to be killed in action during the Second World War, and yet, ironically, it was this war which was to have the most impact on the life of the Denbies estate. The structure of society changed after 1945. The old order had gone: servants were difficult to find, rationing and restrictions had made goods difficult to come by, and costs had soared. The massive Italianate mansion of nearly one hundred rooms which had been built by Thomas Cubitt in 1854 was now impossible to maintain. In 1953 the 3rd Baron Ashcombe took the painful decision to demolish his great grandfather's house and to adapt the adjacent laundry and stableblock into the new Denbies House.

Inevitably the decline in the fortunes of the estate also affected those of the church. The Cubitt family who had for so long been its chief benefactors, defraying many of the church's expenses and bearing the cost of many additions and improvements, could no longer afford to give such support. In addition the decline of the population on the estate had resulted in a dramatic fall in the size of the congregations and the church's income. It was for this reason that the decision to unite the parish of Ranmore with that of Dorking was taken, initially on an experimental basis, when the rector, Revd. N.G. Davies, retired in 1950. The arrangement was that the vicar of Dorking was to act also as rector of

Ranmore. In return the income from the living on Ranmore was to pay for a second curate who, as well as providing additional help at St. Martin's, would also take responsibility for St. Barnabas. The agreement was made permanent in 1958. In 1962, following the death of the 3rd Baron Ashcombe, the patronage of the church was handed over to the Church Commissioners and its final direct links with the Denbies estate were severed.

The Revival of the Church

It might be reasonable to assume that since that time the fortunes of the church on Ranmore have continued to decline, but in fact this is far from true. A small band of loyal supporters fought off all suggestions during the 1960s and early 1970s that it should be closed. Rumour has it that at one point it was suggested it should be turned into a carpet warehouse. Whatever the truth, it was thankfully found that it was going to cost more to keep the church, a Grade II listed building, as a safe ruin than it was to keep it open. Services were cut to once a fortnight and attracted only a handful of worshippers, but gradually the plight of the church and the fight to keep it open became known. With increasing car ownership people were able to come from beyond the parish boundaries, attracted by the church's delightful setting and its friendly atmosphere. Against all the trends, 30 years later the number of services at the church is being increased and the size of the congregation is going up. By the second half of the 1980s major fund raising campaigns were being launched. In addition to raising money both for charity and for projects within the church itself, these have served to give a new community spirit. One of the first of these fund raising campaigns was launched in 1986 to pay for the restoration of the organ.

The Organ and Choir

The organ, like the church itself, is of the highest quality. Built by James Walker in 1859, it was originally situated in an organ loft to the north of the chancel, in what is now the inner vestry. It remained hand blown until 1954 when it was moved to its present position in the north transept of the church. The cost of moving the organ to the north transept was generously borne by members of the Cubitt family in memory of the 2nd Baron Ashcombe who had died in 1947, and his wife Maud. The provision of a new detached console enabled the organist to maintain eye contact with the choir.

Before the Second World War, music had been an integral part of worship at St. Barnabas and originally both an organist and a choirmaster were employed at the church and provided with accommodation on the estate. The choir sang at the weekly mattins and there were regular services of evensong, sung eucharist and even the occasional requiem mass. Membership of the choir averaged about 20, mostly boys with a few men. After the war, however, membership declined and became unreliable, and in the early 1960s the choir was disbanded. Today no formal choir exists at St. Barnabas, but a nucleus of the congregation attend a monthly music practice and lead the singing at services. In addition they sing anthems at special services and form a choir, when requested, to sing at weddings. The annual carol service held at St. Barnabas just before Christmas has become an increasingly popular event, not least because hot mince pies and mulled wine are served in the church afterwards!

The fund raising campaign launched in 1986 raised a sum of nearly £10,000 which paid for an electronic action to be installed in the organ and its specification to be improved. The money was raised, with the help of some very generous donations, by holding a fete, organising a sponsored walk along the North Downs Way from Guildford Cathedral to Ranmore, and serving afternoon teas in the churchyard at weekends. The teas proved to be so popular that they still continue on a regular basis in the summer months. When the work was completed, in June 1988, a special rededication service was held, followed by a buffet supper, held in a marquee in the churchyard, and an organ recital by the organist of Guildford Cathedral, Andrew Millington.

St. Barnabas Present and Future

Another fund raising campaign is shortly to be launched to improve the heating and lighting in the church. Currently, however, work is in progress rehanging and restoring the peal of eight bells at St. Barnabas. Installed shortly after the completion of the church, they were cast by Mears and Stainbank at the Whitechapel Foundry in 1859. In 1910 the original timber beams on which they were hung were found to be rotten and in the following year they were lowered and rehung on steel beams. In 1957 the bells themselves were completely overhauled at Lord Ashcombe's expense, but in 1965 the diocesan architects found evidence that the steel beams on which they hung were corroded, and suggestions were made that the tower of the church might itself be unsound. Since that time the bells have not been pealed although they have occasionally been chimed on special occasions. Throughout this period many people have campaigned to have the bells at St. Barnabas restored, but the necessary funds have simply not been available. However, the work is now being carried out by members of the Guildford Diocesan Guild of Bellringers, whose members have given their time and expertise voluntarily. It has been financed by generous donations from the Diocesan Guild of Bellringers, the Surrey Association of Church Bellringers, the Manifold Trust, and Mr. Adrian White.

Mr. White, who purchased the Denbies estate from the 4th Lord Ashcombe in 1984, has also provided the steelwork and the necessary transport to take the bells to and from the foundry, even though he and his wife are themselves enthusiastic members of the United Reformed Church. And so once again the church has benefited from the generous patronage of the owner of the estate and history has come full circle. Renewed links with Denbies were further strengthened in November 1989 when the 130th Anniversary of the consecration of the church was celebrated with a special service followed by lunch in the sports hall at Denbies. Bishop Kenneth Evans was invited to preach at the service, reviving the old tradition of having a guest preacher on the anniversary of the church's consecration.

The church has also become once more a focus for the Ranmore community. Since the school closed in 1972 and was subsequently converted into a private house, there has been no central meeting place on Ranmore Common, but in recent years the church has fulfilled this role. The Ranmore Residents' Association holds regular meetings in the church and lunches and other social events are held there from time to time. Although Ranmore is now the smallest parish in the diocese of Guildford, with fewer than 100 inhabitants, the members of St. Barnabas church hope to build on these links and see the church go from strength to strength.

Appendix C
Rectors of St. Barnabas, Ranmore

1859-1872	Revd. George Heberden
1872-1899	Revd. Herbert Waddington
1899-1907	Revd. John Henry Hodgson
1908-1912	Revd. Claud Sebastian Harry Sandwith
1912-1923	Revd. H. Roberts
1923-1931	Revd. G.F. Heslop
1932-1936	Revd. W.H.G. Padfield
1936-1937	Venerable W.R. Crichton
1937-1950	Revd. N.G. Davies
1950-1963	Revd. K.D. Evans
1963-1976	Revd. Jack Roundhill
1976-1983	Revd. John Lamb
1983-	Revd. Martyn Farrant

Chapter 9

Pixham Church

Introduction

Many people travel regularly along Pixham Lane without ever realising that there is a church there, despite its facing directly on to the road, for there is no tower or spire to advertise its existence. Yet those who do notice are well rewarded. For this small building, daughter church of St. Martin's, is a beautiful and living monument not only to its patron, Miss Mayo, but also to its eminent architect, Sir Edwin Lutyens.

History

Pixham lies to the east of Dorking at the foot of Box Hill. It is centered around Pixham Lane which links the A24 (London road) and A25 (Reigate road), and crosses the Pippbrook. Its growth was due at first to Pixham Mill and later to its proximity to the Dorking North and Deepdene stations. The Reading line railway arrived in Dorking in 1849 with Deepdene station opening in 1851; the Horsham line followed in 1867 and these had a marked effect on Pixham. They sharply defined the boundaries, altered the placing of the exit to Reigate road, and the Reading line cut the area in two. As yet however there were no houses south of this divide although there had long been a number of large houses plus smaller dwellings to the north, near the mill. In 1860 Miss Ellen Anne Noble (1826-1891) from Boxlands on the London road at the foot of Box Hill, was asked by the vicar, the Revd. W. H. Joyce, to visit the poor of the Pixham district.

She left the area in 1866 to join the Anglican community of nuns at St. Mary the Virgin, Wantage, and Miss Mary Mayo who, with her mother, had in 1862 moved into Riverdale, also on the London road, took over her responsibilities. By 1868 the "poor of Pixham" had swelled in numbers and Miss Mayo, who obviously took her duties seriously, decided that somewhere was needed in which to hold services. As a result when, in that year, a new road, Pixholme Grove, was built, she decided to stand guarantee for the rent of the middle house (the only detached one) and then held evening services there. It was also used as a coffee house and lodging for single men, and the Revd. L. R. Flood (curate from 1875-1884) held bible, confirmation and other classes there.

This sufficed for some time and in 1880 Miss Mayo built a school for Pixham. Then in 1881, forty three plots of land for building were auctioned, and she bought three of them for the use of the church. The land was situated to the south of the dividing railway line and the houses built there formed Leslie Road and Riverside (first called Moleside). Many people from the poorer part of Dorking were re-housed here. The houses were small and mostly terraced and cheaply built. Miss Mayo had certainly realised their significance. "It suddenly struck me that this meant a village", she said in the book that she wrote about Pixham.

In 1883 she was asked by the then vicar, Archdeacon P. R. Atkinson, if he might erect an Iron Room on her land and she agreed. An evening service (held here now instead of at the coffee room), a children's morning service and a Sunday School were held by Miss Mayo and Mr. Flood. As well she ran a Mothers' Meeting here with Mrs. Flood, and night school, twice a week in winter with the curate and "any help we could get". It included a Bible Class, reading, writing and arithmetic, and half-an-hour's recreation; chess, draughts etc.

It was however only in 1890 that the building received a little sanctuary with its altar, ornaments and furniture. The chalice and paten were given by Mr. Arnold of the Grove. On Easter Tuesday of that year the vicar, the Revd. E. A. Chichester, held a dedication service (although the church was not given a name, i.e. it was not dedicated to a saint) and on Low Sunday the first communion service was held. A wooden shanty, which was said to have served as a coffee stall, was erected at the east end.

There were however problems with the Iron Room. Not only was its appearance very ugly, being literally made of corrugated iron, but it was very badly ventilated, far too hot in summer and freezing in winter. It was time for Miss Mayo to show her benevolence once again, by giving her people a "real" church and thereby turning Pixham into a "real" village.

This she did in 1903 when she was "allowed" to give the district a permanent "church room". She commissioned Edwin Lutyens, then a promising local architect, to design it. A special service was held for the dedication on 10 December, 1903, by Canon C. E. Brooke, the vicar of St. John the Divine, Kennington, who was a friend of Miss Mayo. In her book she gave a full account of the impressive service:

"The service, which had been approved by the Bishop of the diocese, began with Hymn 437 (A&M) and consisted of five prayers for the blessing of God on the building, the worshippers, the children who should be taught there, and lastly on the Altar, and on those who should gather round it. It ended with the Collect for All Saints' Day.

Then followed Evensong, which was intoned by the Revd. Basil S. Phillips, the special Psalms were IV, LXXXIV and CXXII; the Lessons, Isaiah LV and Revelation V; the hymns 235, 169 and 305. The sermon was preached by Canon Brooke, who took for his text Genesis xxviii, 16 and 17, 'And Jacob awakened out of his sleep, and he said, surely the LORD is in this place, and I knew it not. And he was afraid and said How dreadful is this place! this is none other than the House of GOD, and this is the gate of Heaven'. By the kindness of the Vicar I was not only allowed to ask Canon Brooke to dedicate the building, but also he and his colleagues, Canon Deedes and the Revd. E. A. Down, both great friends of mine, have often preached at Pixham, and are well known here".

The following week Miss Mayo and her nephew, Mr. C. R. Mayo, gave a commemoration supper. This was limited to the workmen, fathers of the Infant School children, husbands of the Mothers' Meeting members and some who had been present at a similar supper for the school. i.e. men only! No smoking was allowed at the supper but each participant was presented with a pipe as he left. And so, Pixham Church was born.

The Mayo Family

Miss Mayo's father, Charles (1792-1846), born in London, was ordained in 1817 but became known as an educational reformer. He spent three years in Yverdon, Switzerland, where he was English chaplain at Johann Pestalozzi's famous experimental school. On his return to England in 1822 he at once opened a school on these lines in Epsom, where he was helped by his sister, Elizabeth Mayo (1793-1865). In 1826 this school moved to an existing one in Cheam and Charles remained there until his death. The school, which Mary attended and of which her father was a most successful headmaster, is the well known preparatory school still called 'Cheam' even though it has now moved from Surrey. He and his wife, Mary, had three children. The sons, Charles Theodore, (1832-1892) and Theodore, (c1839-1900), both became clergymen. Mary, the daughter, was born in 1834 and stayed with her mother after her father's death. She remained at Riverdale from 1862 until her death in 1933 when she was buried in the family grave at Cheam. In spite of her great age she was said to have remained in good health apart from failing eyesight.

The Mayos were a clerical family and Mary obviously knew several prominent clergymen. Probably as a result of her friendship with Miss Noble, she had stayed with the nuns at Wantage for a considerable period in 1867, when she took exterior vows. She was also an excellent embroiderer. This was a skill which she had learnt from the nuns, who at that time specialised in church embroidery. As an exterior sister she would have been expected to spend some considerable time at Wantage. Her faith was obviously a strong one, with a deep reverence for the sacraments, which she communicated to the people of Pixham, as is shown in the affectionate address made to her on 26 March 1906 by her 'Pixham Mothers', and placed in a service book which they gave her and which is still in the church. There are gaps in what we know about Mary Mayo. These are unfortunate but do help to preserve that air of mystery which seems to surround the lady, of whom sadly no photographs have been discovered.

Sir Edwin Lutyens

Edwin Lutyens was born in 1869, and spent much of his youth in Surrey with local builders, where he gained an insight into the use of different materials. He was soon designing houses all round the home counties, many with gardens by Gertrude Jekyll. The years from 1896 to 1920 are considered to be the period of Lutyens's greatest originality, and within these years lies his design of Pixham Church. Church architecture is in fact rare amongst Lutyens's work. From 1905 his work took him to London, other counties and other countries, and he died in 1944, an internationally acclaimed architect.

Architecture

Just as Miss Mayo wanted, Lutyens's design for Pixham Church was for a church room, a building that could be used not only for worship but also for secular meetings. To this purpose he created one large room, 25ft x 57ft, with a raised platform at the east end. Beyond this a curtain divided the room from the 16ft square sanctuary except during services. To the north side of this main area is a smaller room, 16ft x 20ft with lobbies giving access to the outside, the dais and the main room. The principal entrance at the

Two photographs from Mary Mayo's book, *Pixham 1862-1912*.

The interior of Pixham Church looking east with the cross, vases and candlesticks on the altar which were designed by Edwin Lutyens and have since disappeared, a photograph taken c1912.

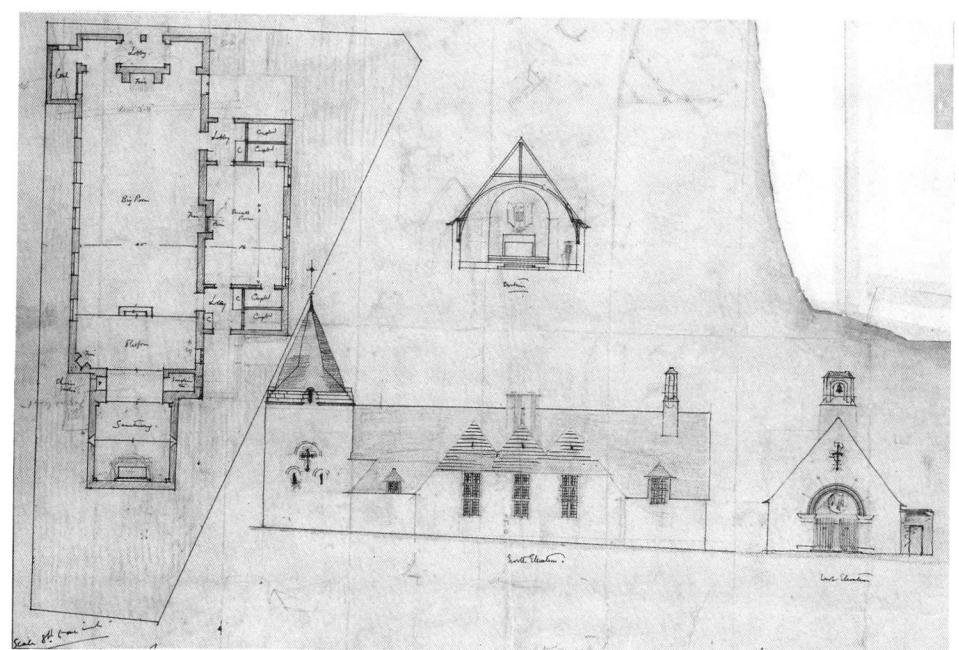

Sketch designs by Edwin Lutyens for Pixham Church, signed and dated January 1903.

Pixham Church choir with the Revd. F. N. Doubleday; the photograph is inscribed 'To Miss L. Fuller the heart and life of Pixham Church', and dated August 1951.

'Godspell' in Pixham Church, 19 June 1987, with the cast singing 'Bless the Lord'.

The service of Holy Communion taken by the Revd. Derek Sayer in Pixham Church on 4 February 1990.

west end leads into a small hall which has two doors into the main room. Again because of its dual purpose, there are no overtly religious features and the key to the architecture is simplicity. The large room, or nave, has a deep barrel vault in white plaster. This rests on a red brick surbase and is interrupted by a series of high brick-built dormer window recesses, six equally spaced on the south wall and two only on the north wall. Between the doors in the north wall is a fireplace over which is a carved stone inscription recording the donation of the building in memory of Mary's brothers, Charles Theodore and Theodore Mayo, and giving the dates of their deaths.

The sanctuary presents quite a different picture. It is covered by a low dome built in chalk, tiles and stone and supported by four semi-circular brick arches. It is one of these which separates the sanctuary from the nave. The other three each contain a window surrounded by trefoil-patterned stonework. The whole effect is masterful and reveals Lutyens's expert knowledge of the use of local materials. The nave is lit by most attractive electric lights, which replaced the original gas lights soon after the church was built. The sanctuary has a circular corona of hand-beaten ironwork, originally made for candles. The simple wooden oak furnishings, including the altar, lectern and chairs, not pews, also date from the church's opening. To suit its dual purpose, there are no fixed furnishings in the main area. In fact to look at the picture of the church's interior taken in 1912 it is hard to see that any changes have occurred.

The exterior of the church is also changed little. It is dominated by the low hung tiled roof, tall gables and chimneys, which are typical of Lutyens's domestic work in Surrey at this date. The walls are of a pale pebbledash giving a good contrast with the roof and with the brick patterns around the windows and on the corners of the walls. But it is the west end which gives a clear indication of the skill of Lutyens, and indicates this is indeed a church. The pair of doors are heavy dark oak over which is a semicircular tympanum of brick and stone with the cross motif set in the centre. Spanning out from this is a pattern in brick with a second cross high in the gable. Above is a bell-turret and at the east end a metal cross stands on the ridge of the roof.

It may be seen, however, from the original sketch plans that it was originally intended that the church should have a spire over the sanctuary at the east end. Various other differences in the windows, gables and doors occur on these plans compared with what was built. Possibly the absence of the spire was due to reasons of economy, but the result is still a beautiful church. The combination of materials, both outside and in, the perfection of the proportions and the contrast between the simplicity of the nave and the complexity of the sanctuary combine to create a masterpiece by Lutyens.

Furnishings

There should be further original fittings, namely an altar cross and vases, all designed by Lutyens and described by him in a letter of 18 August 1903. Miss Mayo also mentioned them in her book and said that they were made of wood, covered with silver leaf and lacquered. They may be seen in photographs, but have now disappeared. They have been replaced by simple wooden ones. Miss Mayo also gave a set of super-frontals and other hangings worked by the nuns at Wantage, which are still in use. Recently these have been supplemented by other frontals and stoles. The organ, built in 1900 for the chapel at

Highgate cemetery, was moved to Pixham in 1964 by John Horley, who was then organist at both Pixham and Ranmore. It is one of the few fixed furnishings. The tiny octagonal stone font on its wooden base is easily moveable.

Rules and Regulations

The trust deed, dated 8 February 1904, and the regulations of the "Pixham Church Room" are copied on a board kept in the church. It was signed by the four trustees: Mary Mayo, William J. Down, A. C. Powell and John Croft Deverell. Mr. Powell and Mr. Down were prominent Dorking citizens who had both been churchwardens at St. Martin's and J. C. Deverell, who owned much land in Pixham, lived in Pixham Firs. The deed placed the use of the building in the hands of the vicar of Dorking and the strict regulations were made for its protection and preservation.

Further rules on two more boards were signed by the vicar, W. T. B. Hayter, and trustees J. C. Deverell, W. J. Down, A. C. Powell and F. P. Down, the latter replacing Miss Mayo. There is no date but Hayter was vicar between 1921 and 1927. The rules were short and precise and forbade, among other things, acting, smoking and dancing. All these rules were little known, (the boards have only recently been rediscovered) and little kept, especially in recent years when they have probably all been broken.

People and Events

Right from its beginning when Mary Mayo decided to build the church, Pixham has lived through the people involved there. A church is its people as much as the building and nowhere can this be seen more keenly than at Pixham.

By all accounts, including her own book *Pixham 1862-1912*, Miss Mayo was a colourful character, the "lady of the Manor", dominating life throughout the area. She always took a strong interest in the goings-on in the school which she had built. In return she gained great respect and every girl would curtsey and boy doff his cap to her. She gave presents to the children; each boy had a blue cape or red tam-o-shanter, each girl a red cape or flannel petticoat. She also held school treats each summer at her home. She seems therefore a strange mixture of the stern Victorian lady, as is shown in the church rules, and a fairy godmother type benefactress.

1890-1920

The early pattern of services held in the Iron Room must be established from the parish magazines, as there are no existing service registers of this period. There was a children's service at 11.00 a.m., and evensong and sermon at 6.30 p.m., and these continued after the opening of Lutyens's church in 1903. It seems clear that the services at Pixham and those at the Cemetery church on the Reigate Road, where there was mattins, sermon and communion at 11.00 a.m. and evensong and sermon at 3.00 p.m., were always intended to be complementary. The service registers of the parish church survive from 1913, and these show that a communion service was irregularly held at 8.00 a.m. on the first Sunday of the month.

The church was served by the curates, but the vicar also came frequently. From the beginning there was a choir, at first led by Mr. Fielder, then by Mr. Gilligan, who staged fund-raising performances at the Oddfellows' Hall. There was also a popular Band of Hope, a temperance organisation, for the children.

The 1920s

Pixham's own service registers exist from 1921. These show that there was a regular communion service at 8.00 a.m. on the first Sunday of the month, and weekly evensong at 6.30 p.m. These were taken usually by the Revds. James Twist (curate from 1919 to 1927) and Fred Chambers (curate from 1921 to 1922, who lived at 12 Pixham Lane). Canon Chichester, then retired, came frequently until 1925, the year of his death. The children were probably attending the afternoon services at the Cemetery church. The services at the end of the decade were being taken either by the Revds. M. E. Thomas (curate from 1928 to 1929) or C. F. T. Willis (curate from 1927 to 1930).

It was in the mid-twenties that Mr. Butcher, of Leslie Road, became caretaker of the church and he remained as such for twenty-five years. There was also a thriving choir led by Mr. Goode from the 1920s to the 1940s. Boys could start in the choir from the age of five or six and wore cassocks and surplices. They stood on the left side of the platform whilst Mr. Goode played a harmonium by the fireplace on the right.

The 1930s

Throughout the 1930s the pattern of services remained as before. During his period as curate from 1930-1935 the Revd. A. E. Robins took most of them. In 1932 a Mission was held in the parish from 16-20 October. Miss Mayo died on 28 July of the following year aged 98 and 10 months. In 1936 the Revd. Tony Weigall (curate from 1936 to 1939) officiated with the help once more of James Twist who became a licensed preacher in 1928 and continued to live at Dorking.

By this time the next "Pixham Personality" had come on the scene. This was Miss Lillian Fuller, a member of the family who had a butcher's shop in the High Street, who began a Sunday School in the 1930s and continued to lead it until the 1960s. She did a great deal for Pixham in other respects too and more will be heard of her later in this account.

The 1940s

The war years, far from being barren ones for Pixham, were a time of growth and activity, particularly on the social front. The two curates, the Revds. John Mortimer (between 1939 and 1943) and Harry Edwards (between 1940 and 1942) now officiated at services. In September 1941 the children's service was re-started and communion was held twice a month. This however increased to a weekly service in 1942. Each Sunday therefore, there was an 8.00 a.m. communion, the 2.30 p.m. children's service, plus evensong at 3.30 p.m. Congregations were however still small and so John Mortimer, together with the very active St. Martin's Youth Fellowship, consisting of young confirmed members of St. Martin's (all under 25), began in 1943 a drive to increase numbers at Pixham. They undertook to visit every house in Pixham whereupon all were invited to a social evening at the school. (The event was too frivolous for them to be allowed to use the church). The evening was an outstanding success and from it a committee was formed. The idea was not only to encourage people to attend Pixham church but also to organise social activities and visit the sick. Wyn Carr and Marguerite Chalcraft, both still with us, and the latter still very much involved with Pixham, together with Ann Arnold, and Vera Grist, initiated the scheme. The Pixham Fellowship was formed and has continued ever since. 1943 also saw the formation of the Church Committee (called the "Church Council" at its first meeting on 3 November). The vicar, the Revd. Leonard Starey, was the chairman, Ann Arnold was secretary and Wyn Carr, social secretary, Miss Cutbush was the treasurer, Geoffrey Haynes represented the Scouts, and Mrs. Bull, the Mothers' Meeting. The committee made (and still does make) all important decisions, financial and otherwise, for the church.

Meanwhile, during the war, a strong Scout troop, most members of which were evacuees, was attached to the church, led by Geoffrey Haynes, who often took the children's services. Under the direction of John Mortimer, the Scouts interpreted the Christmas and Easter Festivals in drama and pageantry. They also formed a dance band with the delightful name of "The Cherubim" who performed at the church in 1943. From 1944 Miss Fuller occasionally took the children's service. In 1949 and 1950 she took it almost every week.

The 1950s

Throughout this decade the regular pattern of services was a communion service at 8.00 a.m. on the first Sunday of the month, together with a weekly children's service at 3.00 p.m. and evensong at 6.30 p.m. In 1953 a monthly service of mattins at 11.00 a.m. was introduced, and by 1955 this became mattins and communion. During changes in clergy, the Revd. F. N. Doubleday was introduced to Pixham in 1951. He had been a dental surgeon and had taken up the ministry on his retirement. He was at first curate at St. Paul's Church Dorking in 1947, but in the same year was given permission to officiate at St. Martin's. He lived in Dorking (first at Woodcote, Coldharbour Lane, and then at Hartland, Moores Road) for the rest of his life. Despite being very lame with arthritis and having no transport he visited all his parishioners whenever any were ill or troubled, and he did so by taxi. Between 1953 and 1957 the children's service was regularly being taken by L. E. O'Hagan.

The 1960s

From 1960 Pixham was again served by the curates although Mr. Doubleday continued to officiate occasionally until 1969. From October 1964 there was a weekly communion service at 8.00 a.m. and evensong at 6.30 p.m. The children's services increased to two a week in 1960 and 1961 when an additional one was held at 10.00 a.m. with Miss Fuller regularly taking the afternoon one. However these and the Sunday school ended for a number of years when Miss Fuller moved away in 1970.

Although the Pixham Fellowship was still strong, their social functions consisted only of a once-weekly game of whist, (held in the vestry) for many years. When Miss Pat Hill, from Downs View (sister of Miss Barbara Hill, both of whom became "Pixham Personalities"), joined the Fellowship in January 1966 she suggested that other functions should be planned and so from 1967 monthly coffee evenings were held. These included slide shows, coach trips, Pixham Entertains, and in 1969, the start of Carols by Candlelight, for their December meeting. For the first two years this evening of carols was held in the vestry and 20 or so attended, but in 1971 the numbers had grown so that it was moved to the church. It was, however, still a social occasion and not a service and the greater informality that this allowed appealed to many who might not otherwise attend the church. The appeal is as strong today and it is an annual event looked forward to by many in and around Pixham.

Throughout its history Pixham has had a choir, but recently it has met only for special occasions. In the 1960s it was led by John Horley and at last Pixham gained an organ given by John in 1964. There were about 22 in the choir at this time. During the 1960s garden parties, organised by the Fellowship, were held annually in September at Pixham End (Friends' Provident Life Office).

The 1970s

During the early 1970s Pixham was made the special responsibility of the Revd. Glynne Owen (honorary curate from 1969 to 1975). One of his actions was to re-start children's services. Holy communion was now held weekly at 8.45 a.m. and evensong once a month at 6.30 p.m. The new family service was monthly and held informally with the children contributing much of the material. The choir, now all female, and led by Miss Doris Smeed, sang only at evensong. After Glynne Owen left services were often taken by retired clergy including Canon Leyland Bird and John Halsey.

The 1970s also saw the rebirth of Sunday School at Pixham. It was taken by Miss Barbara Hill, recently retired, and now living next door to her sister Pat, in Downs View. She had been a teacher and her posts included one at Pixham School in 1947. The Sunday School met after the communion service each week and it was very well attended.

In 1977 a number of essential repairs to the church were needed, including the rehanging of the front doors and the replacing of the stone-work above them plus new window frames and drain pipes. The cost of all these repairs was put at £3000. Pixham church had 17 months in which to raise the money and did so in 12. Also in 1977, one of the founders of the Fellowship, Wyn Carr, left Pixham. She had been sacristan and chairman of the Fellowship and a regular figure at all events and as such was much missed. In 1978 Pat Hill suggested that a tea was held before the harvest evensong service. On further consideration, it was decided to have it after the service, and so the Harvest Suppers began with everyone contributing some food.

1978 also saw the start of the Pixham Junior Drama Group, although it was not so named until 1979. Lynn Parnell, from Downs View, helped at the Sunday School and despite being in the midst of her O-levels she suddenly decided she wanted to stage ''Joseph and the Amazing Technicolor Dreamcoat'' in the church using the Sunday School children. Neither she nor they had any experience but the production went ahead and ''Joseph'' had two performances to packed audiences in October 1978. For Lynn it was planned as a ''one-off'', but the children had other ideas and so they went on to stage a nativity play that Christmas . . . and numerous other productions ever since. From 1979 they have tried to give an annual 'Pixham Entertains' coffee evening for the Fellowship.

Another event in 1978 was a special service and supper to celebrate the 75th anniversary of the opening of the church. The potential congregation at Pixham had increased greatly since the 1950s with the building of a number of new roads and houses; Swan Mill Gardens in 1958, Downs View in 1960, Redcote in 1964 and Chester Close in 1978. Leslie Road has also been extended.

The 1980s

Of all decades, the 1980s probably saw more changes at Pixham than any other. Many of these were instigated whilst David Cleeves was curate between 1985 and 1987 and he was aided in his ideas by a new younger group in the Pixham congregations. It was at this time that Doris Smeed retired as organist and John Philpott took over. The result was more music in services but the demise of the choir. More modern music was introduced, often with guitar accompaniment from Adrian Taylor. The children's services had stopped in 1975 when Glynne Owen left, and, after a period of experimentation, a family service with communion began once a month. Indeed David, with the help of others, did much for the youth of Pixham. Sunday School became Junior Church with a regular rota of leaders; Sandy Horvath aided by Nick and Sara Evans, began a much needed Youth Club to which youngsters from a huge area came. This group, Pixham People, was soon complemented by Junior Pixham People run by Jan Dymond for the younger children.

By this time another "Pixham Lady" had emerged into the forefront; Marguerite Chalcraft had lived in Pixham in her childhood, her brothers had been in the choir and she had continued to worship at Pixham when they moved to Fairfield Drive. On her retirement she returned there and by the 1980s seemed to be running Pixham church almost single-handed, something which, as its only churchwarden, she continues to do. Whatever occurs, Marguerite is there to help. In the early 1980s she began a group for very young children which became known as the Saturday Club.

In 1983 it was realised that the state of the roof had deteriorated and it was decided to re-tile it. However it was then realised that more than re-tiling was needed, and a great deal of money. A roof committee was set up to try and raise the £15,000 needed. This consisted of three members from St. Martin's: Don Parker, Barry Collins and Margaret Millard, and three from Pixham: Pat Hill, Marguerite Chalcraft and Vera Obey. A new roof was provided during 1986 but only after a lot of hard work and help from many sources, including a major grant from English Heritage.

Pixham's contributions to the 1987 Mission were a Flower Festival and production of "Godspell", both held on the same weekend. "Godspell" was very well received, but most important was the profound effect it had on those who took part, both children and adults. Adrian Taylor was Jesus and his calm performance with his very real deep faith behind it was central to the overall feeling of togetherness. Since then the drama group's links with the church itself have been much stronger and they often take an active role in services.

Anthony Anderson as curate in 1988 continued the work David Cleeves had started and the younger generation were well catered for in all respects. In 1988 Sandy Horvath held the first "Jesus Birthday Party" on Christmas Eve. Again this looks like becoming an annual event. There are also many meetings held at the church for the older generation, including 'Pixham Kitchen', a lunchtime café once a week in the vestry.

Services settled at a weekly communion service at 9.30 a.m. (now Rite A after much discussion), with the 4th Sunday in the month designated a family communion. Servers, mostly school children, were introduced and there are now two at every service, robed and trained. Holy communion is also celebrated every Wednesday at 9.45 a.m. (Rite B). Evensong is still held monthly, at 4.00 p.m. in the winter months and at 6.30 p.m. for the rest of the year. Every few months there is a more informal evening service "Family Praise", started by Sandy Horvath, and usually led by him.

The Future

The 1980s did indeed see numerous innovations at Pixham, but, despite a number of the younger set leaving the area, most continue into the 90s under the guidance of assistant priest, Derek Sayer.

And 1990 could be our most exciting year yet because in April we celebrated the 100th anniversary of the church. On Low Sunday 1890 the dedication service for the Iron Room was held. Since that time "Pixham" has grown and blossomed and become the centre of a lively community. And now at last the church has its own name. No doubt it will live on as "Pixham Church" in the minds of many, but it will be called "St. Mary the Virgin", a name bestowed upon it on 22 April by the Bishop of Guildford during the celebrations. And what better name could there be than that shared by our Lady and the patron of Pixham, Mary Mayo. The celebrations included special services, concerts, an exhibition and a pageant.

And so Pixham thrives. We may have broken most of those original regulations, but the spirit of Pixham remains as it has always been. It continues to keep a balance between the sacred and secular whilst combining the two on many occasions and in many ways. Often, as with the harvest suppers for example, it starts a trend to be "copied" by St. Martin's. Jack Roundhill once said "what Pixham does today, St. Martin's does tomorrow". But perhaps the best compliment paid to the church was that by Bishop Russell White:

"Pixham knows how to combine worship and fellowship".

Let that be our continuing maxim.

Chapter 10

The Shared Church from 1976

Following Jack Roundhill's time there was a period not only of consolidation but of significant development in the sharing between the Anglican and the Methodist churches at St. Martins. Shared worship, as has been noted, was at the evening services on Sundays, and a shared Holy Communion was held quarterly. The Revd. John Lamb and the Revd. Bill Murphy agreed that the Eucharist at festivals should also be shared. A shared Family Service on the second Sunday of the month was also instituted. Initially it was planned to let this replace the Parish Communion at 9.30 and the Methodist Worship at 11 a.m., and in consequence a service of Holy Communion was provided at 6.30 p.m. on these Sundays. However, popular pressure from the Anglican congregation led to the reintroduction of the 9.30 Parish Communion on the second Sunday while the 11 o'clock service continued as a shared Family Service.

The Family Service has been important in appealing to those on the fringe of the life of the churches; so increasing commitment and eventual Confirmation became the aim of providing such non-structured worship. Confirmation preparation became a joint venture, and indeed the Confirmations themselves came to be shared. They were conducted jointly by the Anglican Bishop and the Methodist Chairman of District, and confirmees were made members of both churches as a result. This development has contributed a great deal to the growth of the relationship, particularly in terms of the youth work and other groups at St. Martin's.

Happily this has been the case in the development of the Crypt Club on Monday evenings (meeting underneath the church) and the Junior Youth Club on Fridays meeting in the Christian Centre. Both clubs are open to all young people in the area, and the leaders are members of the Anglican and Methodist congregations. On Sundays the Sunday School, called Seekers Finders, has developed into a joint venture, meeting both at 9.30 and 11 a.m.

Another important development in John Lamb and Bill Murphy's day was the growing together of the organisational life of the two churches. From the beginning, the Joint Church Council was the legally constituted body regulating the life of the Shared Church. The actual administration, however, was done by the PCC and the Methodist Church Council meeting separately. On an experimental and informal basis, shared council meetings began to take place, and these proved so popular and successful that the so-called "Combined Church Council" came into being. It met formally for the first time, some months after John Lamb had left the parish, on 14 April 1983.

May 1983 saw the institution of the Revd. Martyn Farrant as Vicar, and with the enthusiastic support of Bill Murphy an "open church" policy was adopted. Owing to vandalism St. Martin's for some years had been open for services and at other times only when volunteers were in attendance. In practice, this meant that the church was usually locked most of the time during the week. With the busy Christian Centre next door it

Harvest Festival at St. Martin's with the Revd. John Lamb and the Revd. Bill Murphy.

The Induction of the Vicar of St. Martin's, 7 May 1983, from left to right the Revds. Ian Fenton and John Silk, Bishop Kenneth Evans, the Revd. Martyn Farrant, Archdeacon Peter Hogden, the Revd. Bill Murphy and churchwardens Len Berry and Norman Gibbs.

View of the Christian Centre seen from the south porch of the church, a photograph taken April 1990.

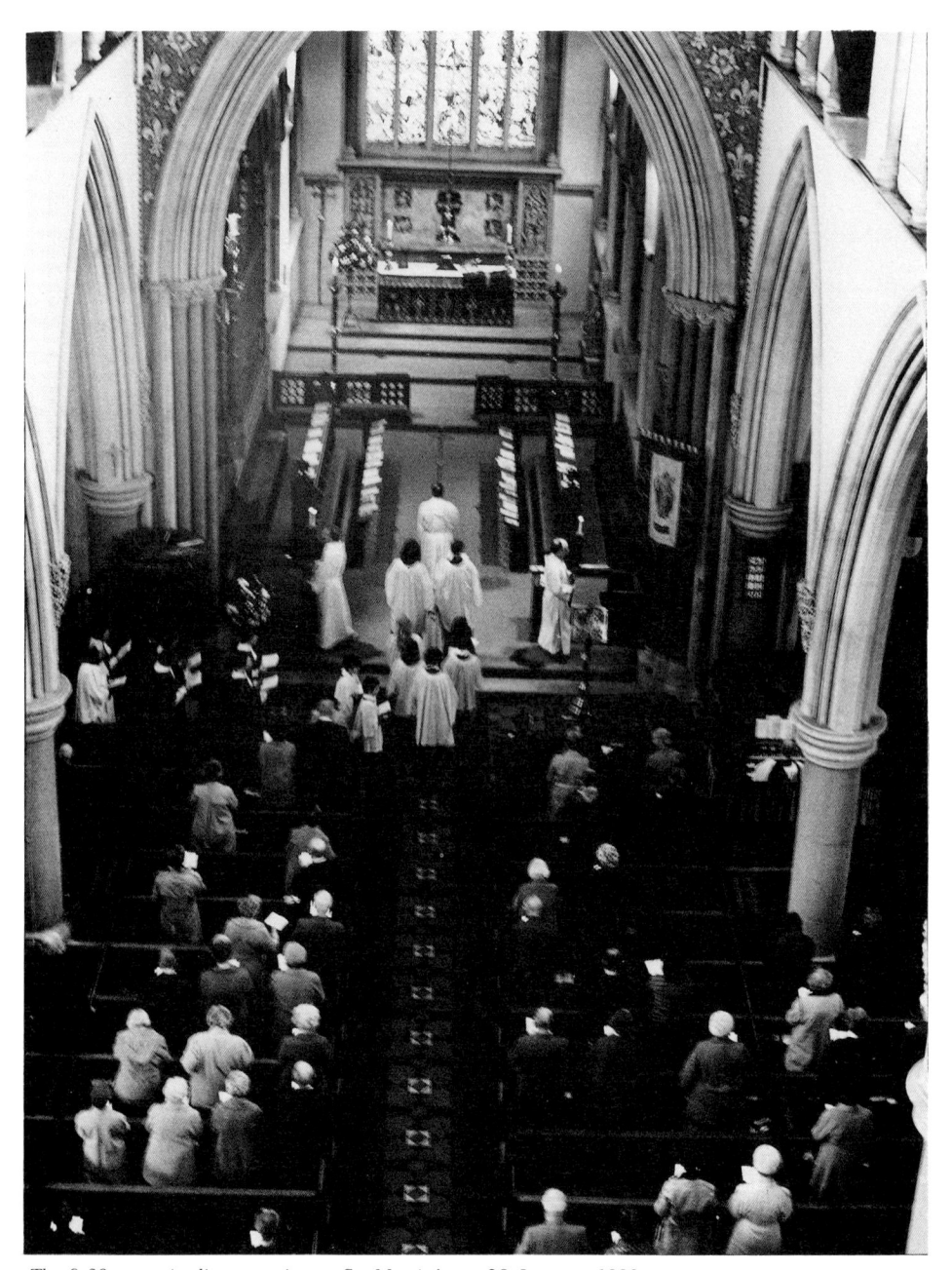

The 9.30 a.m. Anglican service at St. Martin's on 28 January 1990.

seemed curious to the new incumbent that spiritual needs were less easily satisfied at St. Martin's during the week than social and material!

Alongside the opening of the church during normal "working hours" every day, a daily Eucharist was instituted and came to be valued by an increasing number of people. The overall attendance on weekdays has doubled in seven years.

In May 1984 the first stewardship campaign was undertaken on a shared basis. All the planning and preparation, the publicity material, the training of the visitors and their commissioning, and the suppers were carried out as a joint venture. In the main however the visitors visited members of their own denomination, and the resulting monies were assigned to the funds of the appropriate church. The campaign was reckoned a great success both on the basis of the offers of involvement in terms of time, talents and money, and also as an excellent example of the growing cooperation between the two churches.

This proved to be the last major event in the life of St. Martin's in which the Revd. Bill Murphy participated, because in August he moved to Northwood. He was succeeded as Minister of St. Martin's Methodist Church and Superintendent Minister of the Dorking and Horsham Circuit by the Revd. John Hope, who came from Ruislip. In his turn the new Minister worked to extend and consolidate the shared work and witness of St. Martin's, not least in a major event in the life of the town in 1987.

In June of that year St. Martin's Church, along with all the other churches in the town, took part in the Mission to Dorking. A busy programme of events, spanning four weeks, included special activities for children, a pageant of "The Dorking Christian Story" with major contributions by no fewer than seven local schools, a presentation of the life of Christ in words and music, a series of lectures on the Christian life (including one given by the new Bishop of Oxford), a "Come and Sing 'Messiah' " and a youth concert for mission. The opening dedication and commissioning service for all the 24 local churches taking part in "Mission '87" took place at St. Martin's, and the closing event, a day of celebration was held at Meadowbank. During the month of mission St. Martin's, along with all the other churches, delivered a copy of the Gospel according to St. Mark to every house.

The Mission to Dorking, as far as St. Martin's was concerned, was a wonderful experience not only because it brought the Church and the things of God before a very large number of people, but because it moved the Shared Church into ever deeper mutual cooperation and commitment.

An example of this has been the growing relationship between St. Martin's Church in recent years and the churches of the London Borough of Newham. This has resulted in a sharing of interest and concern as well as the giving of financial support to the Community Renewal Programme and the Harold Road Centre. Consequently St. Martin's has benefited from mutual visits and increased awareness of inner city life. All this has given a focus to the work of the churches in their fund-raising for the Anglican Church Urban Fund and the Methodist Mission Alongside the Poor.

A significant part of the life of St. Martin's Church has been the choir. Miss Rosemary Field resigned as Organist and Choirmaster to take up her appointment as Assistant Organist at Birmingham Cathedral and in September 1986 the vacancy was filled by Mr. Martin Ellis. Like Miss Field, the new organist was a musician of great distinction but Mr. Ellis was also a Methodist Lay Preacher. So inevitably began the process of integrating the choir of each church at St. Martin's and all the musical skills under one head. St. Martin's has long had a musical tradition: this has in recent years been strengthened and developed as a feature of the Shared Church.

Another aspect of the Shared Church situation has been the close cooperation between the clergy, and the warm friendship between them that has resulted. And that friendship and trust have been both reflected and encouraged by the increasingly warm relationships between all God's family at St. Martin's. So much so that it is increasingly difficult to notice, let alone emphasize, the difference between an Anglican and a Methodist!

The 11.00 a.m. Methodist service at St. Martin's on 28 January 1990.

The start of the Shared Service of Holy Communion on 25 March 1990, taken by the Revds. John Hope (right) and Martyn Farrant (left).

Appendix I
Vicars

1318	Henry de Habitone	
	Thomas Everard	resigned 1324
1324	John de Arderne	
1349	William de Blakelond	
Fl. 1355-71	Walter Chapman	
	Roger	died 1378
1378	John Appeltone	
1384	William Crese	
1391	Stephen Blancombe	
1403	Robert Ketene	
1404	Henry Ketene	
1413	Robert Cumlyn or Gamlyn	
Fl. 1428-35	Richard Clyff	
Fl. 1445	Henry Carpenter	
Fl. 1448	John Marshall	died 1474
1474	Thomas Fowler	
1488	Thomas Osborne	
1512	Richard Boys	died 1517
Fl. 1520	Miles Hagg	dead by 1530
Fl. 1536	Nicholas Nicolls	resigned 1551
1551	John Glover	
1572	Stephen Richman	
1611	John Crayford	
1622	Paul Clapham	
1624	Samuel Cozens	
1661	Thomas Lea	resigned 1668
1668	Thomas Lea Jnr.	
1705	Henry Lodge	also Rector of Mickleham
1745	Philip Walton	also Rector of Mickleham
1767	Samuel Gooding	
1800	George Feachem	
1837	James Joyce	
1850	William H. Joyce	
1870	Philip Hoste	
1874	Peter R. Atkinson	
1885	Edward A. Chichester	
1921	W. Thomas B. Hayter	
1927	Edward J. Newill	
1936	Oswald A. Hunt	
1943	Leonard Starey	
1949	Kenneth D. Evans	
1963	Jack Roundhill	
1976	John R. Lamb	
1983	Martyn J. Farrant	

Appendix II
Curates or Assistant Clergy

Fl. 1541	Ralph Kyrkham	
Fl. 1632-6	Joseph Biggs	
Fl. 1636	Samuel Wickham	
Fl. 1658	Edward Nabbs	resigned 1661
Fl. 1663	Thomas Langrish	
Fl. 1723	William Vaughan	
Fl. 1725-9	Ezekiel Mills	
1735	Robert Webster	
1737	R. Graham	
Fl. 1746-59	Thomas Turner	
Fl. 1759	Robert Deane	
Fl. 1761	John Lind	
1761	William Scott	
1763	George Allen	
Fl. 1792	Thomas Taylor	
Fl. 1792-4	Joshua Fell	
Fl. 1794	W. Fell(?)	
Fl. 1794-8	George Feachem	
Fl. 1796-1802	Joseph Ogle	
Fl. 1798	T. Ash	
Fl. 1798	J. Taylor	
Fl. 1802	R. Thorpe	
Fl. 1803	J. Hardcastle	
1805	T. Woodroofe	
1814-5	J. T. Lamb	
1814-5	W. Parish	
1815-6	W. Harness	
1816-7	H. Jeffries	
1829-36(?)	George Henry Feachem	
1832-4	R. J. Ellis	
1835-8	Stephen Isaacson	
1838-43	James Wayland Joyce	
1842-8	William Henry Joyce	
1843-50	G. A. Ward	
1850	G. H. Turner	
1851-3	Geldart John Evans Riadore	
1853-6	George Alfred Oldham	

1856-7	G. Witherby
1858-9	W. Tancred
1861-5	H. Bowmer
1866	George Robert Adam
1867-9	Joseph William Chadwick
1869-70	J. N. Nicholson
1871-4	Henry John Gepp
1873-85	Geoffrey Hughes
1874-5	Claude Hankey
1874-5	Edward Buckmaster
1875-81	Henry Walter Brock
1875-6	James Barclay Joyce
1875-84	Luke Robert Flood
1881-2	Francis Kohler Povah
1881-6	Leonard Hedley Burrows
1884-8	Reginald Charles Lott
1886-9	Alexander Thomas Kirkpatrick
1886-9	John Waller
1888-91	Malby Crofton Brownlow
1889-92	John Talbot Godfrey
1889-98	Arthur Selwyn Patterson Blackburne
1891-2	Henry Percy Gocher
1892-5	Henry Roberts
1892-5	Chapman Carey Taylor
1896-8	Mark Napier Rice
1896-1903	Edwin Harding Eland
1898-1900	Arthur Cyprian Moreton
1899-1903	Robert Home
1900-11	Basil Sidney Phillips
1903-4	John Finlay Matthews Duncan
1904-7	Thomas Gardner Devitt
1904-10	Gerard Kerr Olivier
1907-10	Edward Thornton Gotto
1910-28	George Adams
1910-2	Robert H. Freeman
1911-3	Neville G. J. Stiff

1914-5	Leslie E. Burgess
1914-6	Norman King
1915	Graham W. Clitheroe
1916-7	John Rhodes
1917-8	William G. Price
1919-27	James F. Twist
1920-2	Earle McGowan
1921-2	Frederick H. J. C. Chambers
1927-8	Hubert W. Harcourt
1928-9	Morgan E. Thomas
1928-30	Charles F. T. Willis
1930-5	A. Edward Robins
1933-6	Arthur E. Jaggs
1935-7	Bernard A. Whitehead
1936-9	Anthony F. Weigall
1937-40	Alexander G. Dawson
1939-43	John L. Mortimer
1940-2	Henry J. A. Edwards
1943-7	R. W. Anthony (Tony) West
1946-9	David J. P. Llewellyn
1950-4	Peter D. M. O'Beirne
1954-6	Richard (Dick) Jeans
1956-8	Donald Atkinson
1956-60	Cyril Munt
1959-63	Richard H. P. Watson Williams
1960-3	Douglas A. Tatham-Thompson
1963-6	A. Norman Kelly
1964-5	Roger D. W. Hawkins
1966-8	William (Bill) H. McLees
1968-74	Colin de F. Tickner
1974-7	David J. Williams
1977-80	John P. B. Wynburne
1980-4	John A. Silk
1985-7	David J. Cleeves
1988	Anthony Anderson
1989-	Derek J. Sayer

Appendix III
Churchwardens

This appendix is arranged in the following manner: each year indicates the date of election or appointment at the vestry meeting held in or about March or April. Thus 1968-71 means that the two wardens there mentioned were elected or appointed at the vestry meetings in 1968, 1969, 1970 and 1971 and served until the vestry meeting in 1972.

1581-2	Hugh Mason	John Hooker
1631	Ralph Dalton	
1646	John Wood	William Arnold
1672	Sir Adam Browne	Robert Newman
1674	Ambrose Browne	James Mitchell
1730	H. March	J. Goodgroom
1731	J. Goodgroom	
1732	J. Goodgroom	J. Clowson
1733	J. Goodgroom	S. Dendy
1734	T. Carter	T. Dibble
1735	N. Dean	B. Ryley
1736	N. Dean	E. Heathfield
1737	J. Snow	E. Heathfield
1738	J. Snow	R. Simmonds
1739-40	R. Pinney	W. Yates
1741	J. Perkins	J. Stout
1742	J. Wickenden	M. Hall
1743	J. Gurnett	M. Hall
1746	E. Ansell	R. Rose
1749	T. Dibble	
1753	John Carter	W. Round
1754	E. Round	T. Carter
1755	J. Pigott	
1757	J. Perkins	T. Philps
1758	J. Manwaring	T. Philps
1759	J. Clark	T. Philps
1760	J. Attlee	W. Martyr
1761	R. Alloway	J. Clark
1762	G. Dewdney	J. Clark
1763-4	N. Edmonds	W. Risbridger
1765	E. Lambert	W. Risbridger
1766		W. Risbridger
1767	T. Brian	E. Mugridge
1768	T. Brian	J. Sanders
1769	W. Dewdney	J. Sanders
1770	P. Cooke	R. Rose

1771	J. Marshall	J. Franks
1772	M. March	E. Ansell
1773	F. Lea	James Cheesman
1774	F. Lea	E. Bond
1775	G. Rook	E. Ansell
1776	G. Gurnett	W. Dewdney
1777	T. Stout	E. Ansell
1778	S. Dendy	G. Dewdney
1779	J. Attlee	W. Risbridger
1780	G. Dewdney	W. Dewdney
1781	R. Stiles	John Cheesman
1782	P. Cooke	John Cheesman
1783	E. Millett	R. Piper
1784	E. Millett	G. Dewdney
1785	J. Willeter	R. Hills
1786	P. Cooke	M. March
1787	J. Willeter	C. March
1788	J. Willeter	E. Stilwell
1789	E. Ansell	E. Stilwell
1790	John Martyr	E. Stilwell
1791	John Martyr	H. Niblett
1792	John Martyr	James Dewdney
1793	J. Parks	James Dewdney
1794	M. March	James Dewdney
1795	G. Lane	James Dewdney
1796	S. Dendy	James Dewdney
1797	W. Wells	James Dewdney
1798	E. Ansell	J. Willeter
1799-1800	James Rudge	J. Stedman
1801-2	John Cheesman	J. Attlee
1803	John Cheesman	S. Fuller
1804	John Cheesman	J. Wright
1805	S. Dendy	H. Niblett
1806	A. Dendy	H. Niblett
1807	John Cheesman	James Dewdney
1808	T. Piper	John Martyr
1809	T. Piper	W. Wells
1810	H. Niblett	G. Dewdney
1811	W. Lister	G. Dewdney
1812-3	W. Lister	James Dewdney
1814	W. Lister	W. Piper
1815-6	W. Lister	J. Attlee
1817-8	W. Lister	W. March
1819-20	W. Lister	J. Worsfold

1821-3	W. Lister	E. Stone
1824-5	W. Lister	W. Herbert
1826	J. Marshall	J. Niblett
1827-8	J. Marshall	J. White
1829	W. Alloway	James Cheesman
1830	R. Attlee	James Cheesman
1831	T. Hubbard	J. Philps
1832	P. Cooke	R. Greaves
1833	P. Cooke	W. S. Fuller
1834-6	John Rudge	W. S. Fuller
1837	James Martyr	James Cheesman
1838	J. Niblett	William Cheesman
1839	J. Niblett	R. Attlee
1840	J. Niblett	James Cheesman
1841-2	James Dewdney	J. Bartlett
1843-4	James Dewdney	J. King
1845-6	James Dewdney	J. Philps
1847-8	R. Attlee	J. Philps
1849-51	J. Bartlett	J. Philps
1852-3	G. Curtis	W. Latter
1854-5	G. Curtis	J. Ede
1856	W. T. Butler	P. L. Saubergue
1857	W. Latter	P. L. Saubergue
1858-9	W. Latter	T. Davey
1860-1	W. Latter	T. Wood
1862-3	W. Latter	T. Young
1864-6	W. W. Clark	F. Durant
1867-70	J. D. Down	W. J. Rossiter
1871	A. Powell	W. J. Rossiter
1872-5	F. Durant	W. J. Rossiter
1876-7	A. J. Ede	W. J. Rossiter
1878-80	W. Attlee	W. J. Rossiter
1881-4	A. Crofts Powell	F. Durant
1885-7	C. A. White	F. Durant
1888-9	C. A. White	W. Saubergue
1890-1	W. J. Down	W. Saubergue
1892-5	W. J. Down	G. Scales
1896-7	W. J. Down	H. T. Challacombe
1898-1900	G. Gardiner	H. T. Challacombe
1901-2	G. Gardiner	W. Stone
1903-8	W. F. Floyd	W. Stone
1909	T. G. Rix	W. Stone
1910	T. G. Rix	W. J. Brooker
1911-18	J. R. Greenhill	W. J. Brooker

1919-36	G. S. Brown	W. J. Waller
1937-39	G. S. Brown	F. S. Pickford
1940-47	A. W. Tanner	F. S. Pickford
1948-54	C. J. Ivery	F. S. Pickford
1955-64	K. C. Weller	F. S. Pickford
1965	K. C. Weller	J. F. Hunt
1966-67	N. R. Gibbs	J. F. Hunt
1968-71	N. R. Gibbs	C. B. Carr
1972	N. H. Mackereth	N. R. Gibbs
1973	N. H. Mackereth	E. H. Clark
1974-75	C. B. Carr	E. H. Clark
1976	E. H. Clark	N. R. Gibbs
1977-80	R. F. Knott	N. R. Gibbs
1981-83	L. Berry	N. R. Gibbs
1984	D. E. Parker	N. R. Gibbs
1985-89	H. B. Trim	N. R. Gibbs
1990-	H. B. Trim	F. H. Hughes

Appendix IV
Organists

1831-65(?)	Edward James Richard Russell
1865(?)-9(?)	Graham Smith
1869-73	Edwin Augustus Sydenham
1873-4	Luther Marsden
1874-7	George H. Hughes
July 1877-October 1877	Langdon Colborne
October 1877-December 1877	— Wells
1877-1927	Edward Withers
1927-30	Cyril Knight F.R.C.O., Hon R.C.M.
1930-54	William Cole M.V.O., D.Mus.
1954-5	D. J. Wilkes B.A., B.Mus., F.R.C.O.
1955-61	Neil Turner B.A., A.R.C.O.
1961-76	Desmond Swinburn F.R.C.O.
1976-83	Victor Potter
1983-5	Austin Elder (Acting)
1985-6	Rosemary Field F.R.C.O., G.R.S.M.
1986-	Martin Ellis A.D.C.M., F.R.C.O., (ChM)

Since 1973 the Methodist Society has worshipped in St. Martin's Church. Various organists including T. C. Gregory, Peter Essex and the Revd. Norman Goldhawk served the congregation together with Alan Pullinger as Choirmaster until in 1986 Martin Ellis was appointed Organist and Choirmaster to both congregations in the shared Church.

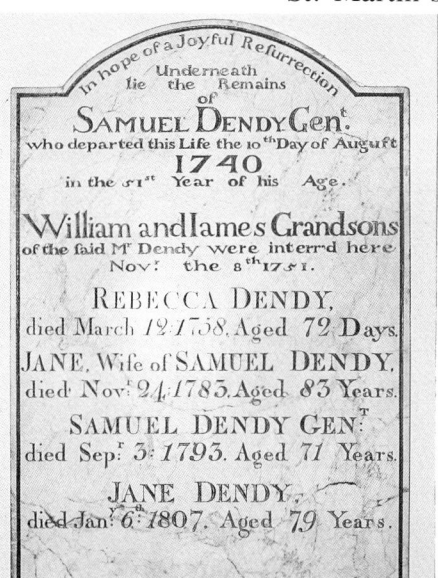

St. Martin's Churchwardens.

Samuel Dendy churchwarden 1733; Samuel Dendy churchwarden 1778.

Arthur Powell churchwarden 1871.

George Smith Brown churchwarden 1918-39.

Churchwardens Norman Gibbs and Ben Trim together with J. E. N. Walker, holding the weathercock from the spire during repairs 17 July 1986.

The present organist, Martin Ellis, 1990.

Sources

Surrey Record Office, Kingston: Post-medieval court rolls, 1649 Survey of Manor, Reports of Charity Commissioners, Salt and 1851 Religious Censuses, Tithe Award, Methodist records and sources.
Surrey Record Office, Guildford: Parish Registers, Service Books, Churchwardens' Returns, Vestry minutes, Tithe papers, Parochial Church Council minutes, papers and drawings on church fabric, furnishing and property, parish magazines etc.
Dorking and District Museum: Sale particulars, newspaper cuttings, parish magazines, directories, pictures and photographs, etc.
Arundel Castle: Medieval manorial court rolls, accounts etc.
British Organ Archive, Birmingham Central Library: Elliot and Hill account book.
Church Commissioners: Boundaries of ecclesiastical parishes.
Greater London Record Office: Records of the Archdeaconry of Surrey, Diocese of Winchester office papers.
Guildford Local Studies Library: Census returns.
Hampshire Record Office: Bishops' Registers.
Museum of London: Whitefriars project.
Pixham Church: Service registers 1921 to date.
Public Record Office: Probate and Exchequer records.
Royal Institute of British Architects Library: Designs by G. G. Scott and E. Lutyens.
Royal Society Library: Bulloch's Roll of FFRS.
Southlands College, Wimbledon: Wesley Historical Society Records.
St. Catherines House, Kingsway, London: Registers of Marriages and Deaths.
Surrey Archaeological Society: Hooper papers, Epitaphs of Surrey, Vol. II (Bax).
Victoria and Albert Museum; Archive of Art & Design: James Powell & Sons of Whitefriars.

Bibliography

Anglo-Saxon Chronicle, ed. Dorothy Whitelock, 1961.
Aubrey, John: *Natural History and Antiquities of Surrey*, reprinted 1975.
Beresford Hope, A. J. B.: *Worship in the Church of England*, 1874.
Blair, John: *Early Medieval Surrey*, 1990.
Brayley, E. W.: *A Topographical History of Surrey*, Vol. 5, [1848].
Brigham, Allan: *'Methodism in Dorking'*, Dorking Local History Group Newsletters 4 & 5, 1976.
Churchill, Winston: *My Early Life*, 1944.
Crockford's Clerical Directories, 1859 to date.
Curnock, Nehemiah (ed): *The Journal of John Wesley*, 1938.
Elphick, Michael: Dorking Local History Group Newsletter 14, 1981.
Hanawalt, B. W.: 'Keepers of the Lights', *Journal of Medieval & Renaissance Studies*, Vol. XIV, 1984.
Hodson, Major V. C. P.: *Officers of the Bengal Army, 1758-1834*, 1927.
Horley, John: 'St. Martin's Parish Church, Dorking, Surrey and its Organs', *The Organ*, No. 186, Vol. XLVII, July 1967.
Joyce, F. W.: *A Life of Rev. Sir Frederick Gore Ouseley*, 1896.
Manning and Bray: *History of Surrey*, Vol. I, 1804.
[Mayo, Mary]: *Pixham 1862-1912*, 1912
[Mayo, Mary]: *Concerning the Three Churches in Dorking Dedicated to St. Martin*, 1917.
Mercer, E. D.: Dorking Local History Group Newsletter 6, 1977.
Peel, Edward: *Cheam School from 1645*, 1974.
Philpott, R. F.: *A Centenary History of the Church and Parish of St. Joseph's Dorking*, 1971.
Purves, Canon J. S.: *Dictionary of Ecclesiastical Terms*, 1962.
Robinson, David: *Pastors, Parishes and People in Surrey*, 1989.
Rose, Charles: *Memories of Old Dorking*, reprinted 1977.
Rowse, A. L.: *The Later Churchills*, 1971.
Shaw, Watkins (ed): *Sir Frederick Gore Ouseley and St. Michael's Tenbury*, 1988.
Stanway, P. (ed.): *History of Pixham School, Dorking 1880-1980*, 1980.
Stenton, Michael (ed.): *Who's Who of British Members of Parliament 1832-1855*, 1976.
Stiff, Revd. N. G. J.: *The Church in Dorking and District*, 1912.
Telford, Rev. John: 'Wesley and his successors in the Dorking and Horsham Circuit' *Methodist Recorder*, 9 July 1903.
Tucker, Brian (ed.): *And Choirs Singing*, 1985.
Victoria County History of Surrey, Vol. 3, 1911.
Westlake, H. F.: *Parish Guilds of Medieval England*, 1919.
Youngs, F. A. Jnr.: *Guide to the Local Administrative Units of England*, Vol. 1, 1979.

Index

(The illustrations and names which occur only in the appendices are not included in this index)

A

Adam, William 19
Addis, Mrs. 39
Advowson, see Patrons
Albany House Home 64
Almshouses 15, 16, 63
Anderson, Anthony 138
Ansell, Edward 52
Archdeaconry 4
Archdeacons 4, 86
Armitage-Smith, Julian 92
Arnold, Mr. 127
Arnold, Ann 136
Arnold, Edward 39
Arthur, Jack 92
Ashcombe, Lord (see also Cubitt) 83, 116
Assizes 18
Atkinson, Peter R. 31, 33, 34
Attersall, Mrs. 97
Attlee, John 92
Attlee, Richard 43
Aubrey, John 4, 19
Auncell, Robert 51
Avery, John 69

B

Baker, Edward 122
Balne, Robert de 11
Baptists 93, 107
Barnes, Mr. & Mrs. J. C. H. 40
Bartlett, John 52
Beard, Samuel 97
Bells 13, 15, 31, 51, 64, 83
Beresford, Lord William 64
Beresford Hope, A. J. B. 69
Beves, Samuel 47, 101
Bird, Canon Leyland 137
Blake, Jack 104
Blancombe, Stephen 11
Bodley, G. F. 39
Bothwell, Samuel 22
Bovill, J. E. 33, 34
Bovill, Priestly Mary 34
Boxall, Charles 53
Bravery, Henry 53
Bravery, Tony 85
Brice, Doreen 84
Brookes, W. McIntosh 21, 22
Brotherhood of the Blessed Mary ... 16

Brown, J. W. 34
Browne, Dr. 31
Browne, Sir Adam 17
Bull, Mrs. 136
Burrow, Henry 33
Burrows, L. H. 62
Burt, Elizabeth (see Forman)
Burt. T. S. 58
Burton, Miss 85
Butcher, Mr. 136

C

Capel, parish of 3
Carr, Wyn 136, 137
Catlin, Robert 51
Cemetery 18
Cemetery Church 18, 135
Census 14, 98
Chalcraft, Marguerite 136, 138
Chaldecott, Charles 61
Chambers, Fred 135
Champneys, Basil 31
Chancel screen 28, 31, 88
Chaplains 12
Chapman, Walter 11
Charities 15, 16, 63, 145
Cheesman, James 43
Chichester, E. A. 1, 31, 62, 135
Chichester family 39, 62
Chitty, Charles 101
Chitty, Jim 92
Chitty, Walter 92
Choir 67, 78, 84, 145
Choirmasters 71, 73, 74, 77
Choral Society 72
Christian Centre 32, 94, 108, 111
Church Halls 31, 93, 94
Church Room 31
Churchill, Winston 64
Churchwardens 14, 153
Churchyard 15, 18, 56, 86
Clapham, Paul 12
Clark, Ted 92
Clayton & Bell 115
Clear, Ethel 93
Cleeves, David 138
Clock 9, 53, 54
Coakes, ... 39, 40

161

Coffee Room 32, 62
Colborne, L. 71
Coldharbour, parish and church 3
Cole, Henry 101
Cole, William 48, 73
Combined Church Council 140
Congregationalism 14, 63
Cooper, Gerald and Liz 93
Corderoy, Edith 102
Corderoy, John 98
Cotton, John Hynde 10
Cottrell, Miss 86, 92
Coulson, John 101
Courtenay, Sarah 19
Cozens, Samuel 12, 17
Crace, J. G. 115
Crawford, William 16, 57
Crypt 18, 95
Cubitt, George 3, 10, 28, 31, 114, 115
Cubitt, Henry 121
Cubitt, Laura 33, 39, 56
Cubitt, Mary 62
Cubitt, Thomas 114
Cubitt Family (see also Ashcombe). 39, 114, 121
Curates 12, 149
Cutbush, Miss 136

D

Dale, William 53
Davies, N. G. 122
Dawson, Catherina 102
Day, June and Michael 192
Dean, Beryl 40
Dedication 4
Deepdene 14, 64, 69
Degenhardt, Charles 104
Denison, W. J. 12, 114
Deverell, John Croft 134
Dewdney, James 52
Dodd, Edward 52
Dodworth, George 61
Domesday Book 4
Dorking Bach Choir 84
Dorking, bishops of 86
Dorking, manor of 3, 10, 14
Dorking Council of Churches 86, 93, 94, 102
Dorking Urban District Council 16, 67
Doubleday, F. N. 81, 102, 136
Doubleday, F. W. 101, 102
Doubleday, Hugh 102
Doubleday, Rosa 102
Down, F. P. 134
Down, W. J. 63, 134
Dymond, Jan 138
Dyson, Ruth 74

E

Edwards, Harry 135
Elder, Austin 77
Elliott & Hill 43
Ellis, Martin 77, 145
Emigrants 13, 15
Essex, Peter. 77
Evans, Kenneth 81, 124
Evans, Margaret 83, 84
Evans, Nick and Sara 138
Excavations 4, 18, 19

F

Farrant, Martyn 140
Feachem, George 21, 22, 52
Fenwicke, Margaret 17, 19, 52
Fenwicke, William 52
Field, Rosemary 77, 145
Fielder, Mr. 135
Finney, John 52
Fishlock, Bernie 95
Flood, Frederick 39
Flood, L. R. 126
Follett, Cyril 86
Forman, Elizabeth 31, 53, 57
Forman, W. H. 27, 57
Forman chancel 27, 40
Forman family 1, 27, 57
Fox, William 16
Frampton, E. R. 122
Friends of St. Martin's Church 85
Frontals 40
Fuller, John 53
Fuller, Lillian 135, 136
Furnishings 9, 32

G

Gardiner, George 19
Gibbs, Evelyn 84
Gibbs, Norman 88, 92
Gilligan, Mr. 135
Glebe 12
Goddard & Sons 28
Goode, Mr. 135
Goodwyn, William 51
Grant, Robert 92
Grant, Thomas 16
Grantham, T. 63
Gravestones 18
Grist, Vera 136
Guildford, bishops of 48
Guildford cathedral 86
Guildford, diocese of 4
Gurnett, George 53
Gurnett, John 53
Gurney, Richard 98

162

H

Hall, John 19
Halsey, John 137
Hamon, John 14
Hardman, John 32
Harrison, James 22
Hart, Thomas 21
Hawkins, Roger 92
Haynes, Geoffrey 40, 136
Hayter, W. T. B. 32, 134
Healey, Tim 92
Hether, John.. 51
Hill, Barbara 137
Hill, Pat 136
Hill, Thomas 14
Hill Norman & Beard Ltd. 46, 49
Hoker, John... 51
Holiday, Henry...................................... 33
Hollier, John.. 52
Holman, Frank 61
Holman, William 61
Holmwood, parish and church 3
Hope, John................................... 108, 145
Hope, Mrs. 3, 153
Horley, John 44, 134
Horvath, Sandy 138
Hoste, Philip 28, 70
Howard, Charles......................... 10, 14, 17
Howard, J. A. 72
Howard of Effingham............................. 10
Hughes, G. H. 70
Hunter, Eileen 91
Hunter, George 92, 93
Hunter, Jim 91, 92
Hunter, Pam 92
Hutton, William 17

I

Infirmary 63
Invalid Kitchen 32, 62
Isaacson, Stephen 21
Isherwood, James 103

J

Joint Church Council 140
Joyce, James 22, 33, 52, 55
Joyce, J. W. 34, 56, 69
Joyce, W. H. 14, 28, 33, 56
Joyce family 33, 56

K

Kaye, Boris 93
Kelly, Norman 92
Kempe, C. E. 39

Ketene, Robert 11
Kingswood, Bert 104
Knight, C.. 73
Knott, Dick 88

L

Lady chapel 31, 39, 43
Lamb, John... 140
Lecturers 12
Leith Hill Musical Festival 74
Lewes, priory of.............................. 10, 11
Lodge, Henry.. 12
Lott, R. C... 62
Loxley, Amos...................................... 101
Lutyens, Edwin 127, 128

M

Malmesbury, John of 11
Markland, Jeremiah 32
Marlborough, Lily, duchess of 40, 43, 46, 64
Marsh, Lawrence 13
Marshall, John 52
"Mayfield" 83, 93
Mayo, Mary 40, 126, 135
Mayo family....................................... 128
McFall, David....................................... 40
McMorran, Donald................................ 83
Mears, Thomas...................................... 51
Memorials................................ 19, 32, 39, 40
Methodists:
 Chapel 96, 98, 110
 Church 17, 102, 111
 Church Council.................. 110, 140
 Circuits 97, 98, 103
 Classes................................... 109
 Manse.................................... 103
 Meeting House 96, 110
 Ministers 96, 97, 98, 112
 Trustees 101, 104
 Women's Fellowship............... 109
Mickleham, parish of 12
Millard, Margaret 93
Mills, Peter 85
Ministers' Fraternal 93
Minster at Leatherhead 3
Missions............... 62, 85, 109, 135, 138, 145
Moore, Hannah (Anne) 27, 57
Moorhouse, J. W. 63
Mordaunt, Viscount 10
Mortimer, John 135
Mothers' Union 84, 93
Mullins, William 13
Murphy, Bill................................ 108, 140
Music 69, 92

163

N

Nelson, John 98
Newill, Edward J. 46
Noble, Miss 40, 126
Nonconformists 14, 18
Norfolk, dukes of 10, 12
North Holmwood, parish and church 3

O

O'Hagan, L. E. 136
O'Neill, (see Chichester)
Opus sectile 34, 39, 40
Organ 43, 104
Organists 104, 138, 156
Ouseley, Frederick Gore 44, 46, 69
Overseers of the Poor 15
Overton family 40
Owen, John 98
Owen, Glynne 137

P

Pancake bell 53
Pantrey, Ron and Margaret 84, 92
Parish clerks 14, 55
Parker, Charles and Mrs. 115
Parlby, George 34
Parnell, Lynn 137
Parochial Church Council (PCC) 16, 86, 87
.... 91, 110, 140
Parsonage, (see Rectors)
Parsons, John 10
Patrons 10, 13, 116
Phelps, Richard 51
Phillips, Basil S. 67, 127
Phillips, J. B. 84
Philpott, John 138
Pickford, Dulcie 84
Pickford, Stanley 83, 92
Pippbrook House 16, 57
Pixham:
  Choir 135, 137, 138
  Church 93, 126, 138, 139
  Organ 133
  School 126
Plague 18
Poole, William 104
Poor Folks Close 17
Poor Rate 15, 16
Potter, Robert 31, 94
Potter, V. 77
Powell, Arthur 28, 33, 34
Powell, A. C. 39, 134
Powell, James & Sons 28, 32, 36, 39

Powell, T. E. 102
Pratt, Chris 92
Preedy, F. 40
Primitive Methodists 107
Pullinger, A. 77
Pullinger, Jean 104
Pulpit 9, 22, 32
Puritanism 13

Q

Quakers 14, 18

R

Ralph, Jim 31, 88
Ranmore:
  St. Barnabas Church 3, 93, 114
  Bells 124
  Cubitt chapel 121
  Charities 121
  Choir 123
  Clergy 125
  Organ 123
  Parish 3, 116, 122
  Parsonage 83
  School 115, 124
Rawlings, Ronald 94, 107
Rectors and Rectory 10, 13
Reformation 10, 13
Registrars 14
Reigate, priory of 10
Rhead, G. W. 34
Richman, Stephen 12
Robert the clerk 11
Robins, A. E. 135
Robins, Will 104
Roman Catholics 14
Rose, Ben 53
Rothes, Earl of 19
Rothwell, F. 46
Roundhill, Jack 86
Roundhill, Marion 87, 88, 95
Rural deans and deanery 4, 9, 18, 28, 62
.... 72, 86, 95
Russell, E. J. R. 69
Russell, William 69

S

Saubergue, P. P. 33
Sayer, Derek 139
Schools 12, 63, 67, 102, 107
Scott, George Gilbert 58, 115
Select Vestry 15
Shared Church 94, 108, 110, 140

Simpson, Norah ... 93
Smeed, Doris ... 137
Smith, Henry ... 17
Smith, Susanna ... 17
Spooner, Miss ... 86, 92
St. Barnabas Church (see Ranmore)
St. Martin:
  Intermediate church ... 16, 21
  Medieval church ... 4, 43, 69
  Present church ... 27, 28
St. Paul, parish and church of ... 3
Stained glass ... 32, 35, 36, 39
Stampe, Joan ... 104
Stapleton, Robert ... 14
Starey, Leo ... 81, 136
Stedman, Beryl ... 93
Stewardship ... 85, 91, 145
Stiff, Neville ... 1, 62
Stillwell, J. G. ... 34
Stringer, John ... 101
Suicides ... 18
Summers, Thomas ... 17
Sunday Schools ... 84, 93, 98, 103, 109
 ... 127, 135, 137
Swinburn, Desmond ... 74
Sydenham, E. A. ... 70
Symonds, Mrs. ... 39

T

Talbot, Catherine ... 19
Talbot, Henry ... 9, 19
Tallents, Stephen ... 55
Taylor, Adrian ... 138
Telford, John ... 103
Thomas, M. E. ... 135
Tickner, Colin ... 92
Tithe barn ... 10
Tithes ... 10, 11
Tower ... 4, 9, 19, 22, 31, 53, 54, 88
Tucker, Abraham ... 32
Turner, N. ... 74
Twist, J. F. ... 81, 135

U

United Methodists ... 107
United Reformed Church ... 86, 94

V

Vaughan Williams, Ralph ... 40, 43, 48, 74
Verger ... 52, 53, 86, 92
Vernon, Norah ... 93
Vestments ... 40
Vestry minutes ... 15, 52

Vicarage ... 12, 55, 83, 91
Vicars ... 11, 149

W

Wade, Judy ... 92
Wailes, William ... 33
Walker, J. W., organ builders ... 44, 46, 123
Walton, Philip ... 12, 52
Wantage, the community of
  St. Mary the Virgin ... 40, 128, 133
War memorial ... 31
Warenne, earls of Surrey ... 10
Warenne, Isabel de ... 10
Warenne, John de ... 10
Warner, Nancy ... 84
Weigall, Tony ... 135
Well ... 13, 15
Well, James ... 101
Weller, Ken ... 92
Wesley, John ... 96, 97
Wesley Guild ... 109
Westcott, parish and church ... 3
White, Adrian ... 124
White, Russell ... 139
White, George ... 91
White, James ... 52
Whitechapel Foundry ... 124
Wilberforce, Samuel ... 3, 28, 31
Wilks, D. J. ... 74
William the clerk ... 11
William the priest ... 11
Williams, David ... 92
Willis, C. F. T. ... 135
Wilner, John ... 51
Winchester, bishops of ... 3, 22, 28
Winchester cathedral ... 3
Winchester, diocese of ... 3
Withers, Edward ... 46, 67, 71
Wode, Richard ... 13
Wolford, Henry ... 13
Woodyer, Henry ... 27, 28
Workhouse ... 15, 16, 17

Y

Young, Carole ... 39
Young, Henry Harman ... 39
Young, John ... 39
Young Wives ... 93, 109
Youth groups ... 84, 85, 92, 93, 95, 104
 ... 109, 136, 137, 138, 140